HOW TO INVEST IN PROPERTY

THROUGH YOUR SELF MANAGED SUPER FUND

2ND EDITION
FULLY REVISED AND UPDATED

Martin Murden

First published in 2011 by Major Street Publishing Pty Ltd
PO Box 106, Highett, Vic. 3190
Contact: info@majorstreet.com.au

2nd edition, fully revised and updated 2014
© Partners Wealth Group Pty Ltd 2014
The moral rights of the author have been asserted

National Library of Australia Cataloguing-in-Publication data:

Author: Murden, Martin, author.
Title: How to invest in property through your self managed
                   super fund/Martin Murden.
Edition: 2nd edition.
ISBN: 9780987542922 (paperback)
Subjects: Retirement income--Australia.
                   Retirement--planning.
                   Real estate investment--Australia--Finance.
                   Real estate investment--Australia.
Dewey Number: 332.63240994

Cover and internal design by Production Works
Printed in Australia by Griffin Press

10 9 8 7 6 5 4 3 2 1

Disclaimer: The material in this publication is of the nature of general comment only, and does not represent professional advice. It is not intended to provide specific guidance for particular circumstances and it should not be relied on as the basis for any decision to take action or not take action on any matter which it covers. Readers should obtain professional advice where appropriate, before making any such decision. To maximum extent permitted by law, the author and publisher disclaim all responsibility and liability to any person, arising directly or indirectly from any person taking or not taking action based upon the information in this publication.

CONTENTS

AUTHOR PREFACE

Since the first edition of this book was published in 2011 much has changed. Australia seems to have largely avoided the recessions experienced by the US and many European countries. Our property market has not suffered the falls in values that have been a consequence of the Global Financial Crisis in so many other economies around the world. We have had three changes of Prime Minister and a change of government. Last, but not least, there have been some changes in legislation that affect the subject of this book: *How to Invest in Property Through Your Self Managed Super Fund*. So I was delighted when my publisher contacted me and gave me the opportunity to revise the book and bring it up-to-date for 2014 and beyond.

Two things have not changed since I first wrote the book. First, is the popularity of self managed superannuation. Current statistics show that there are now approximately half a million self managed super funds (SMSFs) with almost one million trustees managing about one-third of Australia's $1.5 trillion in superannuation! Second, is Australia's long-held fascination with property as an investment. Maybe because it's a tangible asset – you can see it and touch it – or maybe because it doesn't display the vagaries and volatility of the stock market. Many believe, sometimes to their detriment, that property will never decline in value and will always remain the best possible long-term investment.

It is hardly surprising that many Australians who have opted to take control of their own superannuation are interested in including property in their SMSF portfolios. However, direct property investing requires access to substantial sums of money. It was only in September 2007 that the Commonwealth government gave self managed super funds the green-light to purchase property and other assets with borrowings, making entry to the property market considerably easier.

These legislative changes have only been in place for just over six years and there have already been modifications. Despite this uncertainty there has so far been strong interest from trustees of existing SMSFs and other investors looking to set up SMSFs to use their retirement savings to invest in property.

While it is hard to determine exactly how many people have started an SMSF as a result of the legislation, what we can ascertain is that the number of such funds being created has continued to grow in recent years. In mid-2013 it was estimated banks had loaned 30,000 SMSFs a total of $7 billion to acquire property.

And, interestingly enough, not all of these superannuants conform with the traditional SMSF member profile – sophisticated investors, typically professionals, small business owners (but not exclusively so), looking for additional flexibility and control over their super savings.

Instead, many are property investors looking to invest in property via SMSFs and many are people who previously would never have contemplated managing their own fund.

We are seeing people of younger ages than in the past look at using an SMSF as an investment vehicle to fund their lifestyle in retirement.

What they and many others are discovering is that not only is super an excellent vehicle for accumulating wealth and saving for retirement but that purchasing property via super brings with it considerable tax advantages.

Over the 41 years that I have been working with clients on their tax and superannuation, I have never seen such an interest in new legislation. With all new things comes a learning curve. I hope this book will play some part in your self-education as you decide whether investing in property through your self managed super fund is the right path for you.

The book starts by discussing why there is such an interest in self-managed (or do-it-yourself (DIY)) superannuation. It walks you through setting up a fund and then explains the different stages of the fund. Then we take a look at all the options available to investors – buying directly or indirectly; the breadth of property investments; buying with cash or borrowings. Next we consider the tax implications of your investments and make comparisons between investing as an individual, through an SMSF or with partners. The final chapters are concerned with retirement, succession planning and compliance.

Unavoidably there is some jargon associated with superannuation, so we have included a glossary at the back of the book to refer to should you come across a term, concept or abbreviation that you are not familiar with.

Equally as unavoidable are the changes to Australia's tax system. From 1st July 2014, the Medicare Levy will increase to 2 per cent to help fund the National Disability Scheme. The Medicare Levy is quoted throughout the book at the rate at time of writing – 1.5 per cent. If you are reading this book in the financial year 2014-15 and later, you will have to take this increase into account in your calculations.

I hope you find the book useful but, remember, there is no substitute for professional advice from an expert who is familiar with your individual circumstances. Throughout the book I will remind you of this.

Happy reading!

Martin Murden
Melbourne, November 2013

ACKNOWLEGMENTS

My thanks to my colleague, John Lethbridge, for carefully checking the updates to this fully revised second edition.

CHAPTER 1

Why Do-It-Yourself?

ALMOST ONE million people cannot be wrong. At March 2013, according to the Australian Tax Office (ATO), there were 503,320 self managed superannuation funds in Australia with assets of $496,024 million. A total of 958,095 people were members of an SMSF. The most common number of members per fund was two.

These funds represent 99 per cent of all super funds and about one-third of Australia's total superannuation assets.

So, what is it that makes the self managed or do-it-yourself (DIY) approach so attractive?

In addition to providing members with control over how their funds will be invested, those electing to go down the DIY route are generally doing so because it gives them greater investment choice, greater flexibility and lower costs.

Greater investment choice

For the majority of people I have spoken to over my years as an SMSF adviser, the key reason for setting up a self managed fund is because it offers them control and the opportunity to fine-tune their financial future.

Other superannuation funds can offer members choices about how their money is invested. For example, they can take a conservative approach with a high proportion of their savings invested in bonds and cash; or a more aggressive approach favouring international and Australian equities; and there are options in between these two extremes. But with an SMSF you can customise your investment strategy further and decide exactly where, when and how your money will be invested. You have the flexibility to change specific investments when you consider this is appropriate and are not locked into what a fund manager might authorise, potentially resulting in poor returns.

While many trustees (please see glossary at the back of this book for an explanation of this term) of SMSFs may take advice – and many do seek out professional help – the decisions about which investments they will acquire and how they will be managed ultimately are theirs.

Compared with many superannuation funds, an SMSF allows members a broad investment choice. This includes investing in specific direct equities and property, plus a variety of overseas and alternative assets that could even include appropriate levels of collectables or works of art.

With changes to super legislation that are the subject of this book, SMSFs can borrow to buy property and other assets, effectively broadening their investment landscape even further.

Self managed funds do not require set percentages to be invested in a particular asset classes. Rather, they must be invested according to the SMSF's investment strategy as determined by the trustees according to the needs and aspirations of the members (more about this later). And should these change, the strategy can be altered to suit.

Lower costs and taxation advantages

Costs of compliance and administration of an SMSF can be less than the fees charged by a public offer superannuation fund. Although costs will vary with the size of the SMSF (i.e. how much it holds), the level and cost of advice it takes, the number of transactions it makes and the amounts and types of investments it holds.

Investing through an SMSF (or any superannuation fund) provides investors with the opportunity to legitimately reduce tax on investment income and capital gains.

Members pay just 15 per cent in tax on the taxable income in their funds. Compare this with investing in property personally where taxable income is then taxed at marginal rates (up to 46.5 per cent including the Medicare levy).

In addition, provided the funds hold onto assets for more than 12 months, any realised capital gain will be discounted and taxed at an effective rate of 10 per cent on the gain made (more about taxation of capital gains in Chapter 9).

Another key benefit for self managed super fund members is the ability to structure a tax-effective income stream for themselves or their spouses or partners as they transition into retirement and when a member dies. (We will talk about this in detail in later Chapters 12 and 13.)

However, it is important to note that in exchange for these wonderful tax benefits, legislation generally restricts members accessing their super benefits until they have reached 'preservation' age which is currently 55 and will gradually increase to age 60 by 2024.

Who are our SMSF superannuants?

From my 41 years' experience in the industry, DIY super-annuants are generally people who have got considerably more to invest in super than those in industry and retail funds and they are primarily – but not exclusively – small business owners and professionals.

Nationally, the average self managed super fund balance at 31 March 2013 (the latest available figure at time of writing), was approximately $985,000.

As a rule of thumb, SMSFs generally consist of two people – usually a husband and wife or a couple in a de facto relationship. However, the number of male DIYers still outweighs females.

Self managed super fund membership is not restricted to a couple in a relationship and their children. Siblings can establish their own super fund, allowing them to pool their existing account balances for investment purposes.

While more than half of SMSF members are over 55, almost 70 per cent of new SMSF trustees (for funds established during the March 2013 quarter) were aged less than 55 years, with nearly 40 per cent of new SMSF trustees under 45.

Another important part of the SMSF member profile is that those in, or looking at start an SMSF, generally aren't just focused on the here and now. Most have given plenty of thought to retirement. They know when they want to retire, what they will do in retirement and most importantly, how much they will need to maintain their standard of living throughout retirement.

SMSF fast facts

According to the most recent data collected by the tax office, the following facts relate to self managed super funds:

- There are about 503,000 SMSFs in Australia and the number is growing.

- The average SMSF balance is around $985,000.
- Amost 29 per cent of all SMSFs have more than $1 million in fund assets (with 11 per cent holding over $2 million each). Just under 24 per cent had assets of $500,000 to $1 million, a quarter had $200,000 to $500,000 and the remaining group, $200,000 or less (with a little under 6 per cent holding less than $50,000). (These figures are as at 30 June 2011.)
- Approximately 70 per cent of SMSFs have two members, nearly a quarter are single-member funds and the balance have three or four members.
- If you're over 55 and live in New South Wales or Victoria, then you're more likely than any other Australians to run an SMSF.
- With regards to gender balance, females with SMSFs are outnumbered by men, but only just – 52.6 per cent of SMSF trustees are men, and 47.4 per cent are women, generally reflecting that many couples start an SMSF together. In the period since the first edition of this book was published the percentage of SMSF members who are female has increased.

Key Points

- Managing an SMSF offers you greater flexibility and investment choice.
- SMSFs can be less costly to run than public offer super funds.
- All super funds are concessionally taxed, making investing in super very attractive.
- More and more people are seeing the value of starting their own super funds.

CHAPTER 2

Setting up a Self Managed Superannuation Fund (SMSF)

AS SELF managed superannuation has become more popular, the process of setting up a fund has become less complicated. At one time, there was scare-mongering about the costs involved but now the costs for most people (depending on the amount of money you are going to roll over into the fund) are quite reasonable and the procedure is straightforward.

The conversation about whether to set up your own fund will most likely begin with your accountant or financial planner who is familiar with your individual circumstances. They will then be able to manage the process, using the services of experts where necessary. They will advise on compliance, too. However, it is wise to remember that the ultimate responsibility for compliance lies with the trustees.

Some of you reading this book will have already set up your own self managed superannuation fund (SMSF). If this is the case you may want to skip this chapter and move onto the discussion in later chapters about using your SMSF to invest in property. However, you never know, you may learn something from recapping on the basics about setting up and getting a fund started. Also, superannuation and related taxation and compliance matters do change from time to time and may have changed since you set up your own fund.

A self managed super fund is essentially a trust established for one to four people. Here, money is held 'on trust' principally to fund members' retirements. In addition to providing retirement benefits, a superannuation fund can be used to support members should they become permanently or temporarily disabled.

As with any other super fund, should a member die before retiring, proceeds from his or her superannuation account can be used to support family members and/or dependants. Precisely how much is paid out in the event of a member dying or becoming disabled is determined by what has been accumulated. This amount may also be supplemented by an insurance policy payout. You can insure via a super fund against death, total and permanent disability and for income protection.

Ideally the trust deed governing the fund should allow a person who has become totally and permanently disabled the option of taking his/her benefits either as a lump sum, income stream or combination of the two. In the event of death the beneficiary should, if allowed by law, also have the same options available to him or her.

Who can be members of an SMSF?

While membership is open to a wide range of people, there are three important rules governing fund membership:

- No more than four people can be members of an SMSF.

- No member can be employed by another member unless they are related.
- All members must be trustees of the fund or directors of the corporate trustee.

Generally speaking, the majority of SMSFs are established by married couples or couples in a de facto relationship, with single member funds the second most common type of fund.

Are you a candidate for an SMSF?

Before deciding whether to set up an SMSF you need to know what is involved. We have already affirmed that SMSF members have greater control of how their super is invested and managed but what comes with this is a heightened level of responsibility.

Trustees of a fund will determine all investment decisions and will also be responsible for:

- ensuring the SMSF complies with the Superannuation Industry (Supervision) (SIS) laws;
- reporting on member superannuation entitlements;
- preparing annual accounts and reports; and
- lodging annual tax returns for the fund.

Of course, many SMSF members will engage professionals to help them meet these obligations, but ultimately they remain responsible for the smooth operation of their fund and its compliance with SIS legislation.

Those typically engaged to help with the smooth-running of a fund include accountants, fund administrators, superannuation consultants, auditors, actuaries – when pensions or income streams commence – and investment and insurance advisers. For funds investing in property, this list can be extended to include real estate agents, property managers, mortgage and insurance brokers.

While some of these professionals are a must, others will only be required by some funds and for a short period of time.

Although the level of responsibility required of SMSF members may appear daunting, keep in mind that there are over 958,000 Australians who have taken the plunge and manage their own funds – and according to the regulatory authorities, this figure continues to rise every month.

One of the most frequent questions I get asked by clients looking at setting up their own super fund is whether they have enough funds to do so. After all, the costs associated with compliance and management of a fund when measured against your superannuation savings can sometimes make it not worth your while.

Current consensus is that you need a minimum account balance of $200,000 to make setting up an SMSF cost-effective. Some would view this as too low and prefer an opening balance of $300,000. It will depend on a number of factors – your age, your earning capacity and the ages and earning capacities of the other members. There is no legal 'minimum' amount. Funds can be started with less. It is advisable to talk to industry professionals when deciding whether you have adequate super savings to start a self managed fund.

If you are concerned about the commercial viability of your fund once you have rolled over your existing super to your SMSF you can make a determined effort to build up your balance quickly with additional contributions over the next few years.

Setting up an SMSF

There are five key steps involved in setting up an SMSF. They are not overly complex and we explain each in detail below. In essence the steps are:

1. Establish the trust.
2. Decide on a trustee.
3. Elect whether to be regulated by the ATO.
4. Prepare an investment strategy.
5. Open a bank account for the fund.

We then go on to discuss making contributions, taking out insurance and highlight some restrictions on SMSFs.

Establishing the trust

The first thing you are required to do is have a trust deed prepared for your fund. This can be done with the help of your accountant, solicitor, superannuation adviser or a legal services company. The costs involved for this can range from a few hundred dollars to a couple of thousand dollars.

The trust deed must provide details about fund trustees: who they are, how they have been appointed and their powers (i.e. the roles they will play in the management and/or decision-making once the fund is established). It must also set out when and how contributions and benefits will be paid.

The trust deed must be dated and signed by the trustee and a witness, and stamp duty must be paid where applicable. Nominal stamp duty is payable in some states and territories. You can check state government websites for further information.

It is common for the trust deed provider to also provide draft minutes suitable for the initial trustee meeting when the fund is formally established.

Also keep in mind that although your accountant or solicitor will be able to help you establish your SMSF, they cannot provide you with financial advice about investing unless they hold a suitable financial services licence.

If you are setting up an SMSF with a view to investing in property – and possibly borrowing to invest – (and the chances are that if you are reading this book, you are) then make sure you allow for this in your trust deed. It has only been recently that SMSFs have been allowed to borrow. Previously all purchases had to be paid in full up front. So some trust deeds don't allow borrowing. Check with your superannuation adviser to ensure your trust deed allows for the option of borrowing to acquire investments.

Deciding upon on a trustee

To establish the trust, you need to determine your trustee. Generally all the members of an SMSF would be trustees of the fund. A trustee is legally responsible for actions of the fund. He or she will have to ensure lodgement of annual tax returns, preparation of the accounts and having the fund audited annually. Ideally, therefore, they should have a good understanding of business.

The two main options for a trustee are:

- **A member of the fund.** If you choose this option then all members are required to be trustees.
- **A corporate trustee.** This is a separate company that is set up for the specific purpose of managing the SMSF. All fund members must be directors of the corporate trustee.

It is important to point out that trustees cannot be a combination of both individual trustees and a corporate trustee.

As a separate legal entity, a corporate trustee offers some benefit over individual trustees. For example, in the event of a death or divorce, ownership of all of separate SMSF investments, as well as the bank accounts, will have to be changed if the fund has individual trustees. However, for a fund with a corporate trustee, only the directors of the company are altered because the investments are in the name of the company acting as the trustee for the fund.

Should you decide to have fund members as individual trustees, they must be over the age of 18 and cannot be a 'disqualified person'. A disqualified person is someone who:

- has prior convictions involving dishonest conduct;
- is insolvent, bankrupt or has entered into an arrangement with creditors under Part X of the Bankruptcy Act 1996; or
- has a civil penalty order under the Superannuation Industry (Supervision) Act 1993.

Similarly a corporate trustee would be disqualified from being a trustee if:

- a responsible officer (such as a director) was a disqualified person;
- there is an application to wind up the corporate trustee; or
- a receiver or provisional liquidator had been appointed.

A member under the age of 18 cannot be a trustee until such time as he/she reaches the age of 18.

When it comes to selecting trustees, the rules relating to one-member funds and funds with two to four members differ.

Single member funds

A single member fund cannot have an individual single trustee. If you intend to set up an SMSF and be the sole member of the fund you have the following options:

- you can appoint a corporate trustee if you are the sole director of the trustee company;
- you can appoint a corporate trustee if you are one of only two directors of the trustee company with the second trustee being either a relative or a friend;
- you can appoint two individual trustees; you, as the sole member would be one of the trustees and the second trustee would be related (usually your spouse or de facto) or a good friend could be the second trustee.

Example:

Kylie decides to set up an SMSF for the express purpose of purchasing property. As the only member of the fund, her trustee options are:

1. Kylie Pty Ltd, a company of which she is the sole director.
2. Kylie & Brad Pty Ltd, a company with two directors – Kylie being one and her partner, Brad, the other.
3. Kylie and Brad who are individual trustees.

If Brad is to become a member, the first of these options cannot be used.

It is important to remember that no trustee is paid for their duties or services as a trustee.

How does this work out in real life?

Two to four member funds

If you are setting up an SMSF with between two and four

members you have the following options to consider when appointing trustees:

- If the decision is to have individual trustees, all members are required to be trustees and all trustees, members of the fund.
- If it is decided to have a corporate trustee, all members are required to be directors of the trustee company and all directors are required to be members of the fund.

Example:

John and Kellie decide to establish an SMSF for themselves. Their daughter, Ashleigh, who works after school in the family business also joins the fund. The SMSF has a corporate trustee with John and Kellie as the directors. Upon reaching her 18th birthday, Ashleigh is no longer under a legal disability and must become a director of the trustee company.

If at any stage after the SMSF has been established, any individual trustee or director of the corporate trustee believes they could become a disqualified person (possibly as a result of an impending bankruptcy), they should immediately seek advice before getting to that point.

Electing whether or not to be a regulated fund

The next step in setting up an SMSF is to decide whether or not to be a regulated fund. Being regulated by the *Superannuation Industry (Supervision) (SIS) Act* means your fund is eligible for favourable tax treatment. This means money coming into the fund will be taxed at a maximum tax rate of 15 per cent, rather than the highest individual marginal tax rate which currently stands at 46.5 per cent and will increase to 47 per cent after 1 July 2014. Not surprisingly, the vast majority of SMSFs opt to be regulated funds.

You have 60 days from the date of commencing your SMSF to lodge your election (decision) with the Australian Tax Office (ATO). You need to complete an application form to elect to become a regulated fund. This can either be done online **www.ato.gov.au/Super/Self-managed-super-funds/ Setting-up-an-SMSF/Step-9--Register-with-the-ATO/#Elect foryourfundtoberegulated**) or by contacting the information line on 1300 720 092.

After submitting the form, you will be issued with a tax file number (TFN) for the fund and an Australian business number (ABN).

At this point you will also need to determine whether or not your fund will be subject to the Goods and Services Tax (GST). GST is mandatory for an SMSF which derives income from commercial property in excess of $75,000 a year. For all other funds, registering for GST is optional. However, not registering for GST doesn't mean the fund is exempt from paying GST. It simply means your fund will not be able to claim any GST paid and will not have GST included in rental income from a commercial property investment (there is no GST payable on residential rents).

The decision to register for GST should be made after consulting your accountant.

Once you have elected to be a regulated fund the decision cannot be reversed without having to first wind up your SMSF.

Depending on where you source your trust deed (through your solicitor, accountant or superannuation adviser), the election to be regulated may be lodged on your behalf.

Preparing your investment strategy

Fund trustees are required by legislation to have an investment strategy for their fund. Although there is no legal requirement for a strategy to be put in writing, fund auditors generally ask to sight the document, so it is best to have it typed out on hard copy. The strategy doesn't need to be long; many funds operate with just a one-page statement.

When developing the fund's strategy, you must consider the following:

- The *risk involved with, and the potential return from differing classes of investments,* keeping in mind the fund's investment objectives and probable contributions to the fund.

- The *make-up of the fund's investments,* the amount of diversity (initially, and into the future), recognising the potential risk associated with inadequate diversification of investments.

- The *fund's expected cash needs* and the liquidity of the investments to be acquired.

- The *fund's ability to meet any existing and future liabilities* including the provision of benefits upon retirement or at an earlier date.

Recent changes to superannuation legislation mean SMSF trustees also have to consider the insurance needs of the fund members. This does not mean, though, the fund must purchase an insurance policy on the members' lives.

A good financial planner will point out the importance of having a diversified portfolio of investments which leads me to a frequently asked question (particularly important to those wanting to invest in property only), "Do I have to be diversified?"

The answer is that, "No, you don't." You can put everything into property. The decision is yours entirely. Simply, what the law requires is that trustees consider all of the points above concerned with developing a sound investment strategy.

Those funds that do start with just one property and a bank account will find over time additional investments are added. These may be other properties or they could be investments such as shares and term deposits. As trustees for your superannuation fund, the decision as to what your SMSF acquires is yours.

Let's consider the following example.

Example:

Stella and Kevin decide to set up their own SMSF. They transfer their existing superannuation entitlements into their fund and make further contributions which provide them with enough money to buy a property for cash. They have done well investing in property outside of super and feel comfortable and confident investing in this asset class. However, after discussing the matter with their financial adviser they were asked to consider the following.

What happens if either Stella or Kevin die or become disabled? How could a benefit be paid if they were fully invested in property?

To assist in overcoming this problem they could arrange for a term insurance policy to cover each of them against both death and disability. However, as well as and in spite of this, they decided that their fund should be better diversified to cope with any eventualities. They still had the option of borrowing to invest in property and allocating the balance of the fund to equities and cash.

Opening a bank account

The final step in setting up an SMSF is to open a bank account in the name of the fund's trustee(s). In the case of Kylie and Brad (from our first example) and their fund K B Super Fund, if they opted to be individual trustees the bank account would be in the names of *Kylie & Brad* as trustees for K B Super Fund. If there was a corporate trustee, the name of the account would be *Kylie & Brad Pty Ltd* as trustee for K B Super Fund.

Having the bank account in the name of the corporate trustee, with the SMSF also named, ensures the fund's assets are kept separate from their personal assets.

You can open your SMSF's bank account with any deposit-taking institution such as a bank, credit union and building society – or an online account (such as ING or UBank). When you open the account, make sure you ask about:

- minimum balance requirements;
- fees associated with the account; and
- interest rates on earnings.

Most SMSFs only make a handful of transactions each month and as a fund cannot have an overdraft facility, generally there is sufficient money in the account to earn some interest. So make sure you choose an account that will make your money work hardest for you.

Rolling over funds into your SMSF

Having started your own fund, you will now need to transfer or 'roll over' the money from your existing superannuation fund into your self managed fund. Different funds will have different procedures. You will need to either contact your existing fund or if you are using a financial planner, ask him or her for assistance.

A fund is usually required to complete the rollover within 30 days. As soon as the money is in your SMSF account and your investment strategy has been documented, you can start investing.

The fund you are transferring from will want to confirm the money is going to a bone fide superannuation fund so no transfer will occur until after your fund has been issued with its ABN. From July 2013, all rollovers from non SMSFs are required to be made electronically, so the fund from which you are transferring will also need your fund's bank account details.

Making contributions

Making contributions into your SMSF is no different to contributing into an industry fund or a retail fund. There are two types of contributions:

- *Concessional contributions* are contributions using pre-tax dollars. By way of example, this is the compulsory percentage of salary known as the superannuation guarantee (SG) (9.25 per cent from July 2013 and rising to 12 per cent by 2019) which employers have to pay into employees' superannuation funds. For self-employed people and those operating businesses through a company or trust, this is the tax deductible contribution paid as part of your tax planning.
- *Non-concessional contributions* are contributions using after-tax dollars. These can only be made by fund members (not employers).

Concessional contributions (pre-tax)

Members of an SMSF can have their employer pay their compulsory contributions into the member's own fund. A greater amount may be paid by the employer as a result of salary sacrifice arrangements agreed to by the employer and the employee. People who are business owners or self-employed can pay concessional contributions into their superannuation fund themselves. In a handful of circumstances, employees can make concessional contributions on top of those made by employers. However, it would be wise to check with your accountant first.

Concessional contributions are taxed at 15 per cent at the time they go into the fund and are tax-deductible to the individual or company making the contribution. For members with an income of more than $300,000, a higher rate of 30 per cent can apply.

There are caps on the amount you can contribute each year. These are called 'contribution caps'. You should beware of exceeding contribution caps as stiff penalties apply. For the year commencing 1 July 2013, the concessional contribution cap for people aged less than 60 is $25,000 per annum. For those aged 59 to 74 at 30 June 2013, the cap is $35,000.

Non-concessional (after-tax) contributions

These can only be made by fund members (not employers) and cannot exceed $150,000 per annum. However, people under 65 can pay up to three years' worth of contributions – $450,000 – in one year. This means they will be unable to make any more concessional contributions for the next two years. Alternatively, if the person were to make non-concessional contributions in excess of $150,000 in one year, say $180,000 is paid, there are restrictions imposed on the total that can be contributed in the following two years. The maximum that can be paid in this example over the remaining two-year period is $270,000.

Substantial tax penalties apply for exceeding the contribution caps. If you are uncertain as to what you can contribute, check with your accountant before acting. It may save you a lot of unnecessary tax.

I would also point out that it is possible to use personal injury benefits or small business capital gains tax concessions as contributions to your superannuation fund. There are specific rules relating to these contributions and they are excluded from the normal contribution caps. I recommend you seek professional advice before depositing any money into your fund.

People who are in the 65 to 74 age bracket and want to contribute to a superannuation fund must first pass a work test before this is possible. This means completing 40 hours of gainful employment in a period not exceeding 30 days, in that tax year prior to making any contributions. Gainful employment is employment for which you receive an income.

What can't you do with your SMSF?

There are restrictions on what you can do with money in your SMSF. First and foremost, you can't make personal loans to fund members or their relatives – regardless of how small the loan is. It's in breach of legislation and could result in penalties from the Australian Tax Office.

Self managed super fund members sometimes fall foul of this requirement when they're in need of some quick cash.

They grab the first available chequebook without checking and unfortunately this could be the SMSF chequebook! My advice is to clearly mark the SMSF chequebook so there's no risk of making this mistake.

While personal loans are not allowed, SMSFs can make small loans to members' businesses. However, these loans are restricted and at the time of writing this book, it was no more than 5 per cent of the value of the fund.

Unfortunately many people are unaware of these restrictions, while others simply see making loans from the fund as a cheap and easy source of business finance.

It is prudent to never use the super fund for business finance. If your business needs to borrow, go down the normal borrowing path – it's often a much safer option.

When it comes to investing in property, there are some things SMSFs simply cannot do:

- buy residential property from a member or a member's relative;
- allow a member or a relative to live in residential property owned by the fund, such as a holiday house;
- allow a business owned by one or more members to use property owned by the fund without paying rent and having a lease.

Finally, members cannot access funds until they reach 'preservation' age. Currently this is 55 years. However, it will gradually rise to 60 years by 2024.

What about insurance?

If you are establishing an SMSF with the express purpose of purchasing property, before closing your existing super fund (which could be an industry or retail fund), I recommend you seek advice about replacing your insurance cover. As I mentioned earlier, it is now a requirement that SMSF trustees consider taking out insurance for its members.

Typically members of industry and retail funds are provided with insurance cover against death and total and permanent disability. However, when superannuation benefits are transferred out of these funds, insurance cover generally ceases.

Example:

Patrick and Ally, who are members of two separate super-annuation funds, are both insured for $250,000 for death and total and permanent disablement. However, once they start an SMSF and their benefits are transferred across, their insurance cover ceases.

They will need to take out a new policy and provide their chosen insurer with proof of good health prior to a new insurance policy being issued.

Over the years that I have been working in the super-annuation industry, I have come across many cases where people who have lost insurance cover are unable to regain it as a result of health issues arising since the initial cover was granted. When deciding to establish your SMSF, give some thought to your health as it may not be as good as it was in the past.

Another alternative prior to transferring superannuation benefits would be to speak to your existing superannuation fund and establish if it would be possible to have a replacement insurance policy issued which your SMSF could take ownership of.

If given sufficient warning, your financial adviser could ensure your insurance cover is continued across in a policy owned by your SMSF.

If your SMSF borrows to invest you may also want to consider taking out additional insurance to equal the loan liability. This way, should you die, any outstanding debt can be repaid in full.

Your adviser may also suggest an income protection policy. If you are unable to work due to an accident or sickness, part of this income could be used as contributions to your fund to cover any shortfall between the fund's income and its expenses.

Key Points

- To set up an SMSF you need a trust deed and trustees.
- An SMSF must have an investment strategy.
- The SMSF must have a separate bank account.
- You need to consider the different types of contributions and contribution caps as you accumulate funds for retirement.
- Make sure you and your fund have adequate insurance.

CHAPTER 3

Life-cycle of your fund

SUPERANNUATION IS a savings vehicle with the express purpose of providing members with an income in retirement. It is compulsory for most people to have contributions made throughout their working lives, so super is with you for a long time! Depending on your age and current situation, your superannuation will be in one of the following four phases:

- accumulation
- transition to retirement
- retirement
- death.

Yes, it will accompany you through your working life, into retirement and finally its assets are passed on when you die.

The important thing to remember is that you can control each stage of the super life-cycle – and investing for your retirement through an SMSF gives you even more control – to ensure your superannuation works hard for you. We look at how you can do this below.

Accumulation phase

Once you have set up your SMSF, the next step is to increase its balance as quickly as possible. This key phase, when you are accumulating assets and increasing your net worth is, not surprisingly, referred to as the 'accumulation' phase.

The best ways of ensuring your make the most of the accumulation phase are to start early to receive the benefit of compounding; manage your risk so that you don't lose money; and be educated about the investments you are making.

The wonderful thing about being the trustee of an SMSF is that you not only have control over your investment decisions and your asset mix but you have the flexibility to change investments when appropriate. You are not locked into decisions made by others for the benefit of others.

There is a broad array of investment opportunities available to SMSFs. Those of you reading this book are probably interested predominantly in the opportunity to invest in property. However, superannuants also invest heavily in fixed-interest investments and the sharemarket – both in Australia and overseas (see Appendix A).

Superannuation law does not prescribe how much of the fund must be invested in a particular asset or asset classes as long it follows its predetermined investment strategy which can be changed whenever deemed appropriate. However, particularly as you are building wealth during the accumulation phase, you need to consider the risk associated with your investments and how this compares to the probable return.

The key thing about this accumulation phase is that the earlier you start taking your superannuation seriously, the longer the accumulation phase is, and the more money you can put aside in a concessionally-taxed environment to give you a more financially secure retirement. The number of SMSFs continues to grow at a rapid rate and interestingly the latest figures available show almost one in eight new SMSF members were under the age of 34.

You can, of course, just have the compulsory employer contibutions made to your superannuation fund (9.25 per cent of your wages from July 2013). But the accumulation phase is when contributions, both concessional contributions (those using pre-tax dollars) and additional non-concessional contributions (using after-tax dollars) can be made into your fund. Smart SMSF members can work really hard at building up their nest-eggs so that it will provide them with their desired income in retirement.

As you are usually working during the accumulation phase, consideration should be given to your insurance cover, so that should anything unfortunate happen to interrupt this important income stream, such as accident or disability, you will be covered. Worse still, should you become permanently disabled or die, insurance will provide for your spouse or partner and children (as we discussed in the previous chapter).

Transition to retirement

The second phase in the superannuation life-cycle is when superannuation fund members reach 'preservation age'. This is when they can commence an income stream from their fund without having to retire. Preservation age is currently 55 and will gradually increase to 60 by 2024.

For those who are starting to reduce their working hours at this time in their lives, and by implication their earnings, a transition to retirement income stream (TRIS) can be a perfect mechanism to top up income. It also comes with tax benefits.

Initially a TRIS was introduced as a way of assisting people to gradually ease into retirement.

However, some people don't want to reduce their working hours simply because they have commenced a TRIS. So, increasingly, it is being used to top up super as people continue to work full time and put this income back into their super fund, either as a non-concessional (after-tax) contribution or a concessional (pre-tax) contribution using salary sacrifice arrangements. I suggest you speak to your accountant about the options and tax outcomes of transition to retirement income streams.

Where the super fund is concerned, commencing a TRIS provides immediate benefits in that part of the super-annuation fund's income generated – including realised capital gains – is no longer subject to tax.

Where individuals are concerned, for those in the 55 to 59 age group, the income stream will be wholly or partially taxed depending on the individual's circumstances. While we will discuss this in more detail later, in summary your account balance is divided into taxable and non taxable amounts. Payments from the latter are tax exempt while payments from the former are taxable. A tax rebate of 15 per cent will apply to the taxable portion of the income each year.

For those who are 60 or more, benefits paid from a superannuation fund are no longer taxed.

A TRIS is more popular with SMSF members whose account balances are generally larger than members of industry or retail funds.

What percentage of your fund can you take in the form of a TRIS?

Under legislation governing superannuation funds, the maximum amount that can be taken each year is 10 per cent of the member's account balance as at the start of the financial year, or if the income stream is commenced during the year, their account balance at the date it starts.

From 1 July 2013 the minimum members can take is 4 per cent of the account balance at the start of the financial year. If a TRIS commences during the year, the amount used for calculation purposes is the account balance at the time the pension or income commences. The minimum to be paid is calculated on a pro-rata basis based on the number of days to the end of the financial year.

It is important that the commencement of a TRIS be correctly documented. I would suggest you speak to your accountant, financial planner or superannuation adviser in order to get help with this.

Retirement phase

At last – retirement! No more working. Often this is not a one-day event. We have just discovered how you can 'transition' into retirement.

Generally 'retirement' happens when you meet one of the so-called 'conditions of release'. These are requirements that enable you to begin receiving money from your fund without any restrictions. These requirements include having:

- permanently retired from the workforce and reached 'preservation' age (currently 55); or
- reached 60 and have ceased a period of employment; or
- reached 65.

The main difference between the accumulation phase and retirement phase is that fund members or their employers are no longer making super contributions.

On retiring, superannuants essentially have three options about what they can do with their super savings. They can take a:

- lump sum;
- pension or income stream;
- combination of the two.

We look at each of these options below.

Lump sum

Although you can retire at 55 (when you reach preservation age) any lump sum payment you take from your superannuation is only tax-free if you are 60 or over.

For those in the 55 to 59 age group, the lump sum benefit will be divided into taxable and non taxable amounts. The taxable amount comprises pre-tax contributions and the non-taxable amount (or tax-free amount) is made up of after-tax contributions.

People in this age group can receive a **taxable** benefit of up to $180,000 as at July 2013 and **pay no tax** but once this amount has been exceeded, tax will be deducted at the rate of 16.5 per cent. The $180,000 amount is a lifetime figure.

Any investments that have been sold and converted into cash, or any investments that have been transferred to members as part of their benefits, will be subject to capital gains tax (CGT). (We discuss this further in Chapter 9.) These amounts will be deducted before the lump sum is paid.

It is important to point out that you are not required to take an entire account balance as a lump sum benefit and neither is there a minimum that must be taken at any one time. You may decide to withdraw a series of smaller lump sums.

Do keep in mind that if lump sums are taken from the fund and an income stream is not commenced, the fund will remain subject to tax at the rate of 15 per cent on its income each year.

Fund members opting to take their entire account balance as a lump sum often use some of this to pay off debts – such as the mortgage on the family home – investing the balance to provide an income.

It is important to keep in mind that this income from an investment outside of super will be taxed at marginal tax rates.

Pension or income stream

During 'retirement' phase your SMSF can pay you a pension or income stream. This is known as an 'account based' pension and will typically be paid on a monthly basis, with either part or the entire account balance being used to provide an income. This can be supplemented with additional ad hoc payments should a need arise, e.g. you need to buy a new car. The pension can continue to be paid until:

- all the money in the account has been used up; or
- the member dies; or
- the pensioner decides to cease the pension; or
- the 'reversionary' pensioner dies.

A reversionary pensioner is the person you nominate to receive the remaining balance of your pension account should you die. This typically would be your spouse or partner.

Please check with your accountant or superannuation adviser if you want to nominate someone other than a spouse or partner as the reversionary pensioner; this could be a financially dependent or disabled child. There are specific rules as to who can and cannot be nominated. For example, adult children who are not deemed disabled cannot usually be nominated to receive a reversionary pension.

Once all of the fund's members have commenced an income or pension from the SMSF, and contributions are no longer being made, the tax rate for the fund drops from 15 per cent to zero. As an SMSF member, if you are 60 or more, you will no longer pay tax on benefits received.

Assuming there is money remaining in the account once both the member and reversionary pensioner have died, this can be paid to dependants directly or to the estate.

The Federal Government announced in January 2013 that the tax rate for a superannuation fund will remain at nil while pension assets are being realised on the death of a member to enable payment to either beneficiaries or the deceased's estate. Eligible termination payment tax (16.5 per cent of the taxable component) remains payable if the benefit is either paid directly to non tax-dependent beneficiaries or if any amount goes to such beneficiaries via the deceased's estate.

Combination of both

The third option would be to take a combination of lump sum and income stream. The lump sum would normally be used to pay any debts outstanding at the time of retirement or to pay for the new car plus caravan, for example, with the remaining balance being used to provide a regular income in retirement.

Provided the lump sum can be paid in cash without having to sell or redeem investments, there will be no CGT payable. If you are under 60, you may have some personal tax to pay on both the lump sum and the pension (refer above.)

Death

The inevitable fourth phase in the superannuation life-cycle is what happens to your super when you die. I talk about this in detail in Chapter 13, so I shall only make a few brief comments here.

In the context of death, it is important to point out that your superannuation account balance will not automatically form part of your estate. As a result, it is crucial that written instructions be left for the trustee of your fund and that this should preferably be in the form of a valid 'non-lapsing binding death nomination'. This illustrates another advantage of SMSFs. With other types of superannuation funds, a binding death nomination has to be renewed every three years or it lapses.

A non-lapsing binding death nomination is a formal document which enables you to determine who will receive your death benefit (provided they are dependants and/or your legal personal representative). This document effectively binds the trustee into following your instructions in paying your benefits.

Some SMSF trust deeds have been drafted so as not to allow non-lapsing binding death benefit nominations. I would suggest checking your deed and if this applies, to have this restriction removed.

I would also suggest, when drafting your nomination, you obtain legal advice and that, if required, alterations be made to your will. Should you decide to have your superannuation benefit paid into your estate, your will should recognise the source of this money as you may want to specifically allocate your superannuation benefits.

Although we all want to live for a long time, unfortunately

some of us die early. For this reason it is important that in your trust deed your SMSF allows your spouse or partner to take benefits in the form of a pension or income stream, even if you have not commenced a TRIS or retirement pension yourself.

Finally, although your will is not part of your SMSF, ensure this document is kept up to date. This way all your assets will go to the people who deserve them most!

Key Points

- The four phases of the life-cycle of a super fund are: accumulation, transition to retirement, retirement and death.
- The key is to save as much as you can in the accumulation phase.
- A TRIS is a great way of accessing superannuation as you transition into retirement.
- Upon retirement you can take out a lump sum, a pension or income stream or a combination of both.

CHAPTER 4

Direct versus indirect property ownership

ACCORDING TO ATO statistics, the vast majority of the money invested in self managed super funds is invested in the stock market and cash deposits. The opportunity to diversify into property was limited for SMSFs because of its cost. Whereas you can buy parcels of shares for small amounts ($100s or $1000s) to purchase a property you are looking at investing hundreds of thousands of dollars to buy it outright. However, since the changes to legislation to allow SMSFs to borrow money, more retirement savings have been invested in property and this trend is continuing to grow.

The reason for this is probably because investors are seeking capital growth from their investment and property has delivered this growth over the long term. Investing in property through an SMSF has the added attraction of being extremely tax effective.

There have always been two ways of purchasing property via a self managed super fund:

1. directly; or
2. indirectly via a listed or unlisted trust.

Now there is a third:

3. using borrowed funds.

Irrespective of which route you decide to take, your fund will receive the same tax benefits when you sell your investment.

Direct property investments

Making a direct purchase through an SMSF is no different to an individual making such a purchase with cash or with borrowings. It can happen as a result of a private sale or a purchase at an auction. If an SMSF makes the direct investment (i.e. buys the property) with cash, the trustee or trustees have title to the property and, in effect, are the legal owners.

If a husband and wife or a couple in a de facto relationship are the trustees of the SMSF they would hold the title to the property. Or if the trustee is a separate company, the corporate trustee would hold the title.

Note: Although the title of the property purchased directly will be issued in the name of the purchaser, in some states it will not indicate that the SMSF trustee made the purchase. As a result it is common for trustees in these states to complete a simple statement of trust to confirm the purchase was made in their capacity as trustee for the SMSF.

Until 2007, purchasing property directly through an SMSF had only been possible using cash; meaning that the fund had to buy a property outright. Not surprisingly this made investing in property quite prohibitive. Even if a fund could afford to buy a property outright it may have been at the risk of adequate diversification. However, now that SMSFs have the option of using borrowings, this has opened up the opportunity for direct property ownership.

A self managed super fund investing directly (irrespective of whether it is a cash purchase or with borrowings) has the choice of purchasing the property as a sole entity or in partnership with one or more investors.

In Chapter 11 we look at purchasing property with partners. In Chapter 8 we address the specific rules regarding SMSFs using borrowings to acquire investments.

Indirect property investments

For those who prefer a diversified spread of property investments, investing in listed or unlisted property trusts is a likely route. This involves purchasing units in listed or unlisted real estate investment trusts (REITs) (formerly known as property trusts) and does not involve purchasing the property outright. In this scenario, the SMSF is not the legal owner and the title of the property is held by the trustee of the REIT.

Basically, an REIT or property trust is a collective investment vehicle that either:

- owns a portfolio of real property, such as shopping centres or office buildings; or
- was established to acquire a single property.

The latter is often used when the property is too large for a single investor to acquire and a trust may be the best way for the investment to proceed.

Real estate investment trusts are either 'listed' on the stock exchange or 'unlisted' (held privately). We look at both types below.

Listed real estate investment trusts

Some real estate investment trusts are listed on the Australian Securities Exchange (ASX). Self managed super fund trustees can invest in REITs in much the same way as they can invest in shares in a listed company. They can invest directly, via an online broker, (such as Commsec or eTrade) or via a financial adviser or stockbroker.

With listed trusts the buyers and sellers determine the price the units are bought and sold for. As with investing in shares, the price can alter from day to day, depending on supply and demand, economic factors and recent company (or trust) results. Investment purchases should be made in the name of the SMSF trustee.

Example:

Tiffany and Stephanie, who are sisters, are members and trustees of the ST Super Fund. If they purchase units in a trust, these units would be issued to either:

- *Tiffany & Stephanie* as trustees for ST Super Fund; or
- *Tiffany & Stephanie, ST Super Fund account.*

Unlisted real estate investment trusts

Unlisted real estate investment trusts fall into two groups:

- **Trusts established and operated by a financial institution.** In this instance, the units in the trust are issued by the fund manager based on the asset value of the trust and units are redeemed rather than sold to another buyer. However, the fund manager may require notice – possibly 90 to180 days – of the intention to redeem units because money may not be available as quickly as would be the case with a listed trust. With a listed trust, as long as there is a buyer and a seller, the sale or purchase can be made quickly.

- **Unit trusts (created by a group of investors)** for the purpose of acquiring a specific property or properties. These unit trusts typically form when a group of investors come together for the specific purpose of purchasing a property using a trust rather than a partnership arrangement.

Let's look at another example, illustrating the latter scenario.

Example:

Shamiso and three friends decide to buy a commercial property together. They could to do so using a unit trust and assuming the trust was not going to borrow to finance the property, Shamiso could purchase her share through her SMSF.

Regardless of whether they purchase units in a listed or unlisted real estate investment trust, their investment application must be completed correctly.

As the registrar of the real estate trust is required to change ownership of the units to the name of the new purchaser, your financial adviser or stockbroker needs to advise him or her of the name of the new owners (being the SMSF). If you decide to purchase listed REITs via an online broker, you must ensure the account is correctly established in the name of the SMSF and/or the trustees.

Historically there has been a third option – a unit trust associated with an SMSF. This option was typically established for the sole purpose of enabling SMSFs to acquire property using borrowings. This option has been in the main superseded by superannuation funds now being able to acquire property directly using borrowings (but without the need for a separate unit trust).

While existing unit trusts can continue to operate, SMSFs are limited by how much they can invest without breaching superannuation legislation. Any new investment is limited to no more than 5 per cent of the fund's value if the trust is to borrow to acquire property or has existing borrowings.

A word of caution: irrespective of which of the options you choose, it is most important that all documentation provides the name of the correct owner (this should be the name of the SMSF and/or the trustees). If it doesn't, expect your SMSF auditor to request a name change.

Keep in mind that the cost and time involved in executing a change will differ between direct and indirect investments and between states and territories.

Direct or indirect – How do I choose?

When considering whether to invest directly or indirectly and whether to select a listed or unlisted REIT, you need to take into account the following:

- the overall size of your SMSF;
- the size of the investment;
- the SMSF's ability to buy property outright;
- preparedness to borrow to finance the purchase;
- experience with property investment;
- diversification of property investments in your SMSF.

Let's look at each one of these in turn.

The overall size of the SMSF

While there is no set amount you must have accumulated in your fund in order to purchase property directly, it is generally accepted that between $200,000 and $300,000 is the minimum needed to start an SMSF.

However, do keep in mind that there are costs associated with operating an SMSF, such as preparation of accounts and an annual audit.

If you are under the $300,000 threshold, combining your super with your spouse or partner's could help bring the account balance to a more acceptable level.

Basically the larger your SMSF, the better the fund's ability to buy property directly either for cash or with borrowings. A fund with only $200,000 really only has the option of purchasing property indirectly or buying directly with borrowings, whereas a fund valued at $1 million could acquire one or more properties for cash or using borrowings.

The minimum amount required to invest in an unlisted property trust run by a fund manager, can vary from trust to trust. While in theory there is no actual minimum where a listed trust is concerned, in practice the minimum will be based on the value of the units in the trust at the date of purchase and the number of units being offered for sale.

Size of the investment in property

If you are prepared to commit a sizeable dollar amount or a significant percentage of your fund to investing in property, you are more likely to purchase directly.

However, it is generally considered advisable to keep some cash or assets aside to quickly convert into cash for costs associated with the day-to-day operation of the fund. These costs include income tax, accounting and auditing fees, life insurance premiums, if applicable, and property expenses such as rates and insurance.

Example:

Let's take the example of George and Christine. Between them they have superannuation benefits totalling $600,000 in industry and retail funds. They want to use their super to invest in property. They set up their own SMSF and use $500,000 of their combined account balances to purchase property for cash. This does not allow the fund very much diversification but it does leave a considerable amount in cash to meet the financial obligations of the fund.

While fund members can realistically expect rent from their investment property to cover costs associated with managing the property, as property investors they need to plan for the unexpected. A tenant could fall behind in payments or their property could be untenanted for a period of time. Worse still they could have the misfortune of renting to bad tenants who damage the property.

Remember that ongoing contributions are being made to the fund by way of the compulsory employer contributions, payments as a result of salary sacrifice arrangements or personal after-tax amounts and these can be added to the fund's non-property investments. As these amounts grow the fund may decide to acquire another property.

Alternatively, if the fund members choose to keep additional cash or assets outside their fund, they need to be prepared to transfer this to the fund as and when required. However, trustees would need to be mindful about limits on how much they can contribute to their fund in any one year. (Please see Chapter 2 on contribution restrictions.)

Ability to buy property outright

For those funds that have the available cash to purchase a property outright, purchasing directly is a likely route. Before making this decision, consideration should be given to other investments and the trustees' confidence in holding property.

Also keep in mind, there are costs associated with purchasing property. If you have no intention of borrowing to finance your purchase you will need to ensure that the amount of cash in your fund is equal to the purchase price of the property plus costs such as stamp duty, legal fees and rates.

Preparedness to borrow to finance the purchase

For those prepared to borrow via their super fund to invest, they are probably doing so to invest directly into property.

Borrowing to invest in property directly through an SMSF differs from purchasing property personally with borrowings. We go through all these differences throughout the course of this book.

An important difference to consider, when deciding how much to borrow, is that lenders require those investing via their superannuation fund to have a larger percentage of the property's value available as a deposit. This is because under legislation governing superannuation funds only the property being borrowed against can be used as security for the debt. With personal investing, lenders can and do take other property as additional security.

Types of loans and terms are the same irrespective of whether you're borrowing personally or via your SMSF. Loans can be interest-only or principal and interest loans.

Fund trustees need to be able to service loans and will have to allow for increases in interest rates, as well as failure by tenants to pay rent when it's due and an untenanted property.

(Chapter 8 discusses the rules and how to buy property with borrowings.)

Experience with property investment

For those of you with experience in property investment or who are prepared to obtain professional assistance, investing directly may be a preferred option. However, experience goes beyond owning your own home; it means owning at least one investment property outside of your super fund.

While obtaining professional assistance comes at a cost, many have found – whether investing personally or via a superannuation fund – that working with buyers' agents and real estate agents to source properties, mortgage brokers to secure finance and property managers when it comes time to deal with tenants, can save them thousands of dollars.

It's size that counts

While there are many factors which will influence your investment decision, the size of your superannuation fund is the most important.

Using three different fund balances, we will show how the more you have, the greater the number of investment options available to you.

Example 1 – Fund Balance: $300,000

John and Joan decide to start an SMSF with a view to buying property. Because of their small balance they will need to use all their funds to make just one investment while also topping up any shortfall with borrowings.

Example 2 – Fund Balance: $500,000

With this sized balance John and Joan have two options available. They can either:

- use practically their entire fund balance to buy the property; or

- use part of their balance for the purchase and top up with borrowings. What is left behind in the fund can be placed in other investments.

Depending on the amount invested using the second option, John and Joan may be able to acquire a second property, albeit with borrowings.

Example 3 – Fund Balance: $1 million

John and Joan have even more options available to them:

- they could buy a property for cash and invest the balance of their fund in non property investments;
- they could buy two properties for cash;
- they could buy two or more properties using borrowings.

Very importantly, in examples 2 and 3, the decision as to which of the options is to be followed would be John and Joan's.

Before making any decision to invest in property through your SMSF you should seek professional advice. Your investment decisions should take into account a range of factors over and above the account balance in your fund. For example, the ages of the funds' members and their tolerance for risk.

Key Points

- Direct property investing is out of the question for many funds without borrowing.
- Indirect investment is easier with smaller fund balances and it also offers diversification.
- Ideally, you need experience in property investing outside of your SMSF before you borrow to invest through your fund.
- The bigger the fund's balance, the more opportunities you have.

CHAPTER 5

What property you can and can't acquire through your SMSF

THERE CAN be some confusion about what property a self managed super fund can invest in and which are 'no-go' areas. The purpose of this chapter is to provide some clarity on the rules about SMSFs investing in property.

The legislation around self managed super is strict and the penalties for getting it wrong can be harsh. You should always take professional advice when considering how to invest your superannuation in a new area. This book is the perfect primer for you to read before you seek advice, but it is no replacement for expert advice that takes into consideration your specific circumtances.

Basically, there are two distinct rules when it comes to SMSF trustees acquiring property from individuals, couples, companies or trusts; one is relevant to investing in residential property and the other is relevant to investing in business or commercial property.

What SMSFs <u>cannot</u> invest in

RULE 1: Self managed super funds are prohibited from buying residential property from fund members or from people, companies or trusts they are 'associated' with. Purchases must be made at 'arm's length'. While who constitutes an 'associate' is generally pretty obvious, sometimes it is more difficult to determine. A simple test to determine 'association' is as follows:

- **Two people would be deemed associated** if they are related (e.g. family members such as brothers and sisters), or because they are actively involved in a business venture together (such as being in a partnership).
- **A person and a company would be associated** if the person is a director of a private company and is actively involved in the day-to-day operations of the company or if the person owns over 50 per cent of the shares or has voting rights for the company.
- **A person and a trust would be associated** if the person is a beneficiary of the trust and the trust is a discretionary trust (such as a family trust) or if the person owns over 50 per cent of the units or has voting rights for a unit trust.

Where there are doubts about association, I would recommend you ask your accountant, solicitor or superannuation adviser to confirm if your property acquisition is acceptable under superannuation legislation.

Several years ago I was asked by an accountant in a Victorian regional town to advise on a case involving a husband and wife who had acquired property outside their SMSF in their own names. The property was to be used as the new family home. However, instead of selling their existing home the couple arranged for it to be transferred to their fund as an *in specie* (or non cash) contribution.

The solicitor handling the transfer had not queried the legality of the transfer under super legislation nor had the couple (who were trustees of their fund) asked him if the transfer was allowed.

What was clear was that all parties involved were unaware that an *in specie transfer* constituted an actual purchase, although money had not effectively changed hands. In essence, property cannot be transferred from an 'associate' (the fund members) to their fund.

The couple had no option but to sell the property. They could have pooled resources and purchased the property themselves but due to other commitments they were unable to raise the necessary finance.

Another option could have been to transfer the property to the members as a lump sum benefit, but neither qualified to receive a lump sum at that time. They were not yet 65 and were still gainfully employed in their own business.

The fund's auditor was required to issue a qualified audit report and forward a contravention notice to the regulator, the ATO.

What SMSFs can acquire

RULE 2: Self managed super funds can buy 'business real property' from anyone, including fund members or people, companies or trusts they are 'associated' with. They can also buy residential property owned by someone else who is not an 'associate'.

Business real property

To pass the 'business real property' test and be classified as such, the property must be used wholly and solely for business purposes at the time of purchase. It can be a shop, factory, office or farmland. It can even be a house used for business purposes, such as a doctor's surgery or an accountant's office.

Simple? Well it can be more complicated. Let's take a look at an example of where the same piece of property does and doesn't pass the test.

Example:

Sajee and her husband, Sam, own a shop in a suburban shopping strip which they would like to sell to their superannuation fund. If the property was vacant at the time of the sale, it would NOT pass the business real property test because it was not being used as a business. However, if someone was renting the shop and operating a going concern such as a cafe, it would qualify as 'business real property' and their SMSF could purchase the building.

Before transferring a shop, office, factory or farmland which you own personally but are not using for business purposes into your SMSF, make sure you have a tenant running a business from that property or you will fail the business real property test.

Also, when transferring business real property to your fund, it must be bought at an arm's length price. I would suggest speaking to a local real estate agent and asking him or her to give an appraisal of the property's value.

You can purchase business real property from someone previously unknown and once done, lease the property to a business you own. Let's look at another example.

Example:

Erkan and his wife, Sultan, attend an auction and purchase a factory in the name of the trustee of their superannuation fund. After settling the purchase, they lease the property to ES Pty Ltd, which is a business they own.

When you lease the property to either an associated party or an arm's length tenant, a lease should always be drawn up and commercial rent paid, regardless of whether the tenants are members of your fund or not.

Note: If there is an existing tenant the lease must be changed to show the SMSF trustee as the new landlord. Also if your tenant is to pay rent direct to the owners (the fund), your new bank account details will need to be provided.

Residential property owned by someone else

While SMSFs are prohibited from buying residential property from fund members or from people, companies or trusts members are 'associated' with, they can purchase residential property from people and entities where there is no association.

If you are uncertain ask your accountant or superannuation adviser because apart from the potential legal problems it could prove costly to rectify.

Unlike business real property (which can be leased to associates) residential property investments cannot be occupied by fund members or their family, irrespective of how much rent is paid.

This may seem unfair, particularly if family members would be paying the same rental as someone with no association but, trust me, it prevents a lot of heartache.

During my time in the industry I have come across numerous instances where there is no lease and no expectation that rent will be paid, often as a result of members providing their children with somewhere to live. Using the SMSF's assets for this purpose is a serious breach of legislation and fails to comply with another test – the 'sole purpose test'.

To pass the 'sole purpose test' an SMSF's primary purpose is to provide fund members with benefits when they retire, or to provide their beneficiaries with benefits should they die early. If a main purpose of an investment property is to provide adult children with a home, then it fails the sole purpose test.

Reasons for the rules

The rule preventing SMSFs from acquiring property from associates was introduced in the early 1990s when it was discovered that some SMSFs were paying well in excess of the value of the properties they purchased from associates.

At the time, Australia was in the grip of a recession and many businesses, particularly small businesses, were struggling with debtors, creditors and bank overdraft interest rates.

This saw a spate of businesses establish their own SMSFs, with fund members selling investment properties they owned to these newly established funds at inflated prices. This in turn released money transferred from previous super funds, and provided the businesses with a much-needed cash injection.

This activity resulted in legislation banning funds from acquiring residential property from either fund members or associates as well as restricting the acquisition of business real property. The latter ban, however, has since been revoked.

Renting and leasing investment properties

While SMSFs are not legally required to have real estate agents manage their investment properties for them, many fund trustees and individual property investors prefer going down this route.

For many investors, getting a professional to do the job allows them to focus on more important issues such as running their own business.

Speak to any SMSF trustee and they will be convinced that the best tenant for their fund's commercial property investment is the business owned and operated by a fund member.

However, from my experience, this is not always the case.

What I have seen over the years is that leasing to fund members often results in lease agreements which are little more than a single written page and sometimes less and which neglect to spell out the term of the lease, make no provision for rental increases and fail to provide the landlord with any rights in the event of rent not being paid.

Renting to associates can result in irregular rental payments and in some cases no payment at all.

While most landlords accept that late payment can occur from time to time, they would take action if this happened consistently or if there was a complete failure to pay. Basically SMSF trustee landlords should be no different. After all, they need to act in the best interests of fund members.

I'm often asked by clients if there is a way of avoiding these problems. There is, provided of course that you get a professional to manage the process for you. However, if you decide to go ahead and do it yourself, it is important that you view renting to an associate as no different to renting to someone at arm's length.

Following negotiations over rental and lease conditions, the lease should be written up (ideally by your solicitor). This should stipulate:

- the rent – how much and when it is payable and when it will be increased;

- the term of the lease and renewal options;
- the rights and obligations of both the owner and tenant; and
- what will happen if one of the parties fails to fulfil their side of the contract.

Once the lease has been written up, it must be signed by the property owner (you, the SMSF trustee) and the tenant.

In the example below, I have shown how things have the potential to spiral out of control when the fund is the landlord and fund members are the tenants.

I was asked to advise on a problem involving a two-member SMSF and a property it co-owned. The co-owner was a member of the fund. To complicate matters, ownership of the property wasn't equal; the fund had 60 per cent and the member owned 40 per cent.

The problems started with the tenant – a business owned by both members of the fund.

The business had been experiencing difficult trading conditions for three years and rental payments had been spasmodic and were well in arrears.

The member who had 40 per cent ownership of the property decided to take money equivalent to three years' rental rather than her 40 per cent share. As a result, the SMSF was deemed to have 'loaned' money to the member – something which is prohibited. By providing the property to the tenant (the members' business) at what was in effect less than commercial rent, the trustees of the superannuation fund could also be considered to have failed the sole purpose test as mentioned above.

In a case such as this, the ATO could be expected to remove the concessional tax rate of 15 per cent and replace it with the highest marginal tax rate for an individual plus the Medicare levy backdated to when the fund first commenced as a penalty for breaching superannuation legislation. This would have an associated effect in that the employer would be deemed to have failed to comply with the requirements of the superannuation guarantee legislation. It is also possible that the members could be banned as trustees and this may require their fund to be wound up.

Ideally what should have happened?

The landlord (the fund) and the tenant should have stuck to the commercial lease agreement which had been drawn up. Unfortunately, they chose to ignore it.

If they had followed the requirements to the letter, the landlord would have taken action against the tenant, possibly evicting the tenant and finding a replacement.

Although this seems harsh, the SMSF would have behaved no differently with an arm's length tenant.

The fund should also have insisted that the member who co-owned the property only take her share of the rental and not part of the SMSF's income.

Key Points

- SMSFs cannot buy residential property from an 'associate'.
- SMSFs are permitted to buy 'business real property'.
- SMSFs can lease business real property to an 'associate' under an 'arm's length' agreement.

CHAPTER 6

Property choices

WHEN YOU stop to consider the variety of property options available to investors it is hardly surprising that this is a very popular investment asset class. We have already looked broadly at direct versus indirect property investing, in this chapter we review more closely the direct property options and how they might appeal to SMSFs.

While the choice of property available to SMSF investors is surprisingly broad, as the list below indicates, keep in mind that your purchase or purchases are for investment purposes only. They must pass the sole purpose test, that is have the express purpose of generating income and/or capital gains to support you in your retirement. They must also comply with the specific rules regarding property purchases through your SMSF that we reviewed in the previous chapter.

Below we open your eyes to the range of property options available.

Residential

Residential property comprises free-standing homes, flats and apartments – pretty much anywhere that people reside. It is the most popular type of investment property because most investors have already had some experience in buying and selling their family home. They "understand" this type of investment as they have lived in residential properties.

Just so that there is absolutely no confusion I will state here:

Self managed super funds are expressly forbidden from investing in the family home.

There, it's even emphasised in bold type, so we can take this in and move on. You can forget any fanciful ideas of investing your super in that beach-front property and moving the family in to enjoy the views and the lifestyle!

So an SMSF can buy a residential property for use by people other than members of the fund and anyone associated with the fund. The fund cannot rent the property to family members or relatives, irrespective of how much rent they are prepared to pay.

Another important rule regarding residential property is that it cannot be purchased from fund members or from people, companies or trusts they're 'associated' with. It must be purchased at arm's length from an unassociated third-party.

This book is not a book about property investment per se (there are plenty of good books on general property investing) but I will make some comment here. Some experts believe in investing in units or flats, others suggest inner-city apartments, and others still believe in buying a three-bedroom home in the outer suburbs or country areas. As I said, this discussion is outside of the scope of this book. I will only say that the choice of which type of residential property you buy will depend upon many factors, including:

- the assets of the fund;
- the extent (if any) to which you are comfortable borrowing;
- the rental income and capital gain you calculate your investment will return over the timeframe of your investment; and
- the costs of maintaining and managing the property over the same period.

Holiday homes

If you buy a holiday home through your SMSF the same rules apply. It must be rented out at arm's length. You cannot buy it with the intention of you and your extended family members using it all year round – even if you pay market rents.

Some of my clients have invested in property through their SMSF and ask me whether upon retirement they can move into it. The short answer to this question is yes. The longer answer requires the property to be taken out of the super fund at retirement. This can be done in one of two ways.

The first option is to transfer the property to the members as an *in specie* lump sum benefit. It is important to check the trust deed governing your superannuation fund allows this.

The second option is for your super fund to sell the property to the members, either before or after they have started taking an income or pension from their fund.

Both taking the property as a lump sum benefit and selling the property to the fund members is a disposal for capital gains tax purposes and I would recommend you speak with your accountant prior to taking action. As stamp duty laws vary across the country, it would be wise to also check on their impact on the decision to take the property out of the SMSF.

Hotel rooms/serviced apartments

Hotel rooms can often be bought by the fund as an investment and then leased to the entity managing the hotel or apartments. As long as these are arm's length investments they might be good investments for your SMSF (depending on your individual circumstances).

Retail, commercial and industrial property

Next we look at property from where businesses are run. There are three main categories:

- **Retail** – including shopping centres as well as individual shops in a shopping strip.
- **Commercial** – offices in the CBD, in suburbs and/or in regional areas.
- **Industrial** – including factories and warehouses.

Many small business-owners and/or professionals running their own practices choose to manage their own superannuation funds. These people are often renting their business premises and so consider the option of buying them through their SMSF.

An SMSF can purchase any of the property types listed above directly from anyone (including fund members or people, companies or trusts they are associated with) but they must pass the 'business real property' test. This means the property must be used wholly and solely for business purposes at the time of purchase (this was discussed further in the previous chapter).

An SMSF can then lease the business real property out to an associated business on a commercial basis.

Vacant land

An SMSF can buy vacant land but it cannot borrow funds to buy to construct or renovate a property. If your intention is to buy vacant land through your SMSF with a view to subdividing and developing it, then this is not allowed. It is recommended you speak to your accountant or superannuation adviser prior to purchasing the land. Undeveloped vacant land will cost your super fund ongoing rates and maintenance charges and may probably not be deemed a sound SMSF investment.

Rural property

Rules for purchasing rural property – which covers a wide range of properties, including vineyards, hobby farms, dairies or primary produce farms – can vary depending on the business and/or the circumstances of your SMSF. Broadly, you can lease farmland from your fund but you should discuss this purchase with your adviser. There are particular rules for buying rural property on which you intend to live and from which you intend to run your business.

Also, if you or an associate owns the land or rural property your fund is looking to purchase, it must pass the business real property test before the fund can acquire it.

Car parking spaces

Quite a popular property investment is investing in a car parking space. Car park owners sell off individual spaces and these can be rented out to companies or individuals or back to the car park owners. The returns from this investment can be quite healthy and the rents are usually indexed for inflation. The cost of entry is quite low compared with other property options.

Buying overseas property

While most self managed superannuants prefer purchasing property in Australia, there are always those looking to invest internationally.

Although these investments have tended to be in countries from where fund members originate or where they intend retiring to, over the last three to four years I have noticed a growing trend in the number of people wanting to purchase residential property in the US. The belief is that property can be acquired there cheaply since the collapse of the US property market and there could be a much greater potential for capital gains.

While investing in the US, or any overseas destination for that matter, may appear enormously attractive, it is important to consider this option with your eyes wide open. The following issues need to be thought through carefully, irrespective of which country you're looking to invest in:

- **Exchange rate** – when you eventually sell the property and the proceeds are returned to Australia, these will come back at the prevailing exchange rate. As a result any profit could well be wiped out by adverse movements in the exchange rate.
- **Local laws** – you need to be across local legislation in the country/state/municipality where you invest and have a good understanding of your rights as a

property owner there. What, for example, are you able to do if your tenant is unable or unwilling to pay rent? Keep in mind that your rights and those of your tenant will differ from country to country.

- **Costs of agents** – you may need to appoint a local agent to manage your property. Finding a reliable one long distance may be difficult and affording his or her costs may adversely affect your investment returns.

- **Taxation** – your fund may be required to lodge an annual tax return in the country in which you have purchased your property. Establish whether this is the case before going ahead with the purchase. I suggest you speak to your accountant and don't be surprised if you're referred to an international tax specialist who can better explain relevant income and capital gains tax rules.

- **Travel costs** – because of language/communication difficulties and differences in property ownership laws, you may be required to travel overseas from time to time to sort out problems which cannot be resolved over the phone or via email. You may also need to inspect your property from time to time. These additional costs need to be factored in when you are weighing up the viable return on the investment as well as the cash flow needs of the fund.

While SMSFs can invest in the same type of properties overseas as they can in Australia, do keep in mind that because these investments are subject to the laws of the country, this could cause complications so make sure you do your homework beforehand.

In keeping with Australian requirements, all overseas investments must be consistent with the sole purpose test which means, for example, a residential property located in the US cannot be leased to a fund member or relative of a fund member.

It is also important that you have documentary evidence that your SMSF owns the overseas property and that your fund ownership is recognised by the country where your asset is located.

In some countries where 'foreign entities' such as a super fund are not permitted to purchase property directly, an agent may be required to make this purchase on your behalf. If so, you must have an enforceable agreement between your fund and the agent. By enforceable, I mean an agreement which will hold up in the courts of the country you've invested in. I would recommend you discuss this subject with your accountant and solicitor before going ahead with your purchase.

If you are investing overseas, do keep in mind that Australian superannuation legislation requires that all records be kept in English. Any document relating to the property, be it the title, the purchase contract and so on, all need to be translated into English. This is the responsibility of the trustee, with the fund bearing any costs associated with translation.

An option worth considering when investing internationally is the use of unit trusts offered by financial institutions. Although these don't give you direct ownership of specific investments, they delegate some of the difficulties and responsibilities addressed above while at the same time providing you with a portfolio of property investments.

Purchasing options

Generally speaking most of the property options discussed above can be acquired either directly by the super fund or indirectly through a real estate investment trust (REIT) or unit trust.

Buying directly means the fund trustees purchase the property with cash or with borrowings, have title to the property and are, in effect, the legal owners.

Purchasing indirectly usually involves the trustee buying into or investing in listed or unlisted property trusts and does not involve purchasing the property outright. In this scenario, the SMSF is not the legal owner and the title of the property is held by the trustee of the property trust.

From my experience in the SMSF industry, shopping centres and city office buildings are generally purchased indirectly via listed or unlisted trusts, the key reason for this being the considerable size of these investments.

However, having said that, I have seen SMSFs purchase offices and car parking spaces using strata title arrangements and then renting these offices to fund members' businesses.

Strata title is a form of ownership devised for multi-level apartment blocks and horizontal subdivisions with shared areas. The 'strata' part of the term refers to apartments being on different levels or 'strata'. Strata title was first introduced in 1961 in NSW to better cope with the legal ownership of apartment blocks. Previously, the only adequate method of dividing ownership was company title which suffered from a number of defects such as the difficulty of instituting mortgages. This term also applies to house type strata title units in Australia.

As for the remainder of property types listed above, the majority are more likely to be purchased directly by the fund itself.

Key Points

- Property offers a range of investment options.
- SMSFs cannot invest in the family home.
- SMSFs can invest in property overseas but extra care and due diligence is needed.
- SMSFs can invest directly or indirectly.

CHAPTER 7
Buying property with cash

THEY SAY cash is king and prior to September 2007 this certainly was the case if you intended investing in property through your SMSF. A self managed super fund could *only* acquire property with cash or as a result of members transferring 'business real property' into their super, a process known in the superannuation vernacular as making an *in specie* contribution.

Although the law has now been modified to enable SMSFs to borrow to invest, people are still coming to grips with the change and in many instances prefer paying cash for their purchases, usually to avoid their super fund going into debt.

In much the same way that individuals purchase residential or commercial property via auctions or private sale, SMSFs can do so too. However, there are the restrictions discussed in Chapter 5.

While individuals need to have cash up front, SMSFs have the luxury of supplementing what is already in the fund with additional 'immediate' contributions. However, it is important these contributions do not exceed the allowable contribution caps discussed in Chapter 2 (currently $25,000 per annum [$35,000 for those aged 59 to 74 at 30 June 2013] for concessional contributions and $150,000 per annum for non-concessional contributions).

Exceeding contribution caps

Unfortunately, exceeding contribution caps can have unpleasant consequences which I'll better illustrate with an example.

Example

Kate has $300,000 in her super fund. She is under 65. In the 2011/12 financial year, she made a non-concessional (after-tax) contribution of $200,000 to her SMSF. She hadn't made any non-concessional contributions in the two years prior.

Kate decides to purchase property in the 2012/13 financial year and discovers a suitable residential property. However, it costs $550,000 which means she will need additional cash to complete the purchase and ensure there is enough money in the fund to cover costs and any immediate maintenance work.

Kate decides to make up this amount with additional non-concessional contributions totalling $300,000.

Unfortunately, she will have a nasty surprise awaiting her when her SMSF accounts are prepared at the end of the financial year. She'll discover she has breached the non-concessional contribution cap by $50,000 and will be liable for a tax penalty.

During the two-year period, she will have contributed a total of $500,000 to her SMSF in the form of non-concessional contributions, taking her over the $450,000 limit, and she will be penalised by having to pay 46.5 per cent in tax on the excess.

In practice the penalty could be much higher – up to 93 per cent. Tax at the rate of 46.5 per cent can be imposed if either of the concessional or non-concessional contributions caps is exceeded. The higher tax rate of 93 per cent would apply if the combined cap for both concessional and non-concessional contributions were breached.

Let's continue with our example.

Example (cont'd)

In addition to her contributions, Kate's employer has made concessional contributions of $25,000, partly to meet the compulsory contribution requirements and partly as a result of salary sacrifice arrangements.

The combined contribution cap in any one year is $475,000 ($450,000 + $25,000) for people aged under 60. A person aged 59 to 64 can have a concessional contribution of up to $35,000 in the 2013/14 year. For those in the 65 to 74 age group the current combined cap is $185,000 ($150,000 + $35,000).

However, as Kate has made non-concessional contributions of $200,000 in the previous year, she has triggered the 'bring forward' provisions and is restricted to a non-concessional contribution of $250,000 in this year ($450,000 − $200,000).

Kate would be subject to tax of between $23,250 and $46,500 depending on her age and the amount of concessional (tax deductible) contributions made to the superannuation fund for her.

Purchasing without money changing hands

Where there is insufficient cash in the SMSF to purchase property, business real property owned by members can be sold or transferred to the fund without cash changing hands. This is called an *in specie* contribution.

To better illustrate how the process works, let's take a look at Marie.

Example

Marie purchased a shop several years ago. The shop is currently being used by Jan to run her pharmacy.

Marie decides to transfer ownership of the shop to her SMSF. This would be a 'disposal' for capital gains tax (CGT) purposes because ownership will be going from Marie to the SMSF. This means she will have to pay tax on any increase in the property value, less the 50 per cent CGT discount (see Chapter 9 for more information on CGT).

Prior to the transfer, Marie must obtain a valuation to ascertain the 'market value' of the property. A real estate agent can provide her with a market appraisal which can be used as the basis for the transfer.

Marie's property is valued at $400,000. Her SMSF has $140,000 in cash and she hasn't made any non-concessional (after-tax) contributions to her fund in the past three years.

Assuming she doesn't want her fund to borrow in order to acquire the property, she has two options available with regards to transferring the property to her SMSF. She could:

- have her SMSF pay her, for example, $100,000 and then make an *in specie* non-concessional contribution of $300,000 to the fund; or
- make an *in specie* non-concessional contribution of $400,000 to the fund.

Marie's decision will be influenced by:

- The amount of capital gains tax she will have to pay personally.
- Stamp duty and other expenses paid by the fund in relation to the property acquisition. In some states an *in specie* transfer to an SMSF does not attract stamp duty. Duty on property acquisitions varies between

states and territories. Your solicitor will be able to advise you in this regard.

- Marie's desire to build up her SMSF account balance.

Regardless of which option she chooses, Marie's SMSF will be able to take ownership of the shop even though there was insufficient cash in the fund to purchase the property outright.

Buying off the plan

With the recent trend in our major cities towards redevelopment of former office property and industrial sites into residential property, it has been a popular approach for developers to sell property 'off the plan'. When purchasing off the plan, you're in essence buying an apartment or house that is yet to be constructed and which is part of a property development.

Depending on the developer's requirements, you may have to pay a deposit, followed by progressive payments. Alternatively, a deposit may be required with final payment due on completion of the property.

I would strongly recommend prior to entering into any contract, you:

- check the contract to determine when progress payments have to be made and the total of each payment; and
- either have sufficient cash in the fund or hold other assets that can be converted to cash in order to make the payments.

Should you decide to take the second option (pay a deposit with final payment on completion), remember our earlier comments about contribution caps should your fund not have sufficient cash to pay the balance of the purchase.

So how does buying off the plan work when an SMSF is involved?

Ideally, the SMSF will foot the initial deposit and subsequent payments will come from either surplus cash already in the fund, other investments that are to be redeemed or sold, or additional contributions you make to the fund. These may be concessional or non-concessional contributions.

While this may all appear relatively straightforward, do keep in mind that issues beyond your control could prevent the necessary payments being made. A prime example of this was the Commonwealth government's reduction in concessional (pre-tax) contributions that took effect from 1 July 2009. In the year prior, people in the 50 to 74 age group could make concessional contributions of $100,000 per year. The very next year, the figure was reduced to $50,000. For people under 50, it dropped from $50,000 to $25,000.

To get an idea of the impact of this on those purchasing property off the plan, let's take a look at the following example.

Example

Peter and Julie used their SMSF to purchase an apartment off the plan in April 2009. Having paid the deposit, a further $500,000 was required once the apartment was completed. This was scheduled for August 2010. Because Peter and Julie were over 50, they decided to each contribute their maximum concessional contributions ($100,000 each) in the 2008-09, 2009-10 and 2010-11 tax years — a total of $600,000.

After allowing for tax on the contributions, this would leave a net $510,000 in the fund.

Unfortunately as a result of the government changes, while the $100,000 in concessional contributions was allowable in 2008-09, only $50,000 each was permissible in the following two years.

This meant they were only able to contribute $400,000 ($340,000 after tax) which would leave them with a shortfall of $170,000. (Note: since the above occurred there have been changes to both contribution levels and personal tax rates.)

What options do Peter and Julie have?

They could sell off other investments in their SMSF. If they are reluctant to do so because of the quality of these investments, they would have to make non-concessional (after-tax) contributions to make up the balance.

However, the problem with making the non-concessional contributions is that they will have to pay tax at marginal rates on the money earned prior to making the contribution. If they're both on the highest tax rate, this would mean having to increase their combined personal income by an additional $317,757, and after deducting $147,757 in tax, they would finally arrive at the required $170,000.

A lower gross amount would have been required if they were in a lower tax bracket.

Who exactly is the 'buyer'?

The buyer of a property is the fund's trustee, not the fund.

However, there are differences from state to state and the territories about how the name will appear on the title. Here's an example to illustrate just how this can vary.

Example:

Greg has his own SMSF called *Greg's Super Fund*. It has a corporate trustee, Greg Pty Ltd. The purchaser of the property is Greg Pty Ltd in its capacity as trustee for Greg's Super Fund.

Depending on the state and territory, the contract note and contract will either show the purchaser as:

- *Greg's Super Fund;* or
- *Greg Pty Ltd ATF Greg's Super Fund;* or
- *Greg Pty Ltd as trustee for Greg's Super Fund.*

Given these variations it is not unusual for the incorrect name to be used on documentation.

In states where the name of the SMSF is not shown on the title, trustees are often required (by SMSF auditors) to draft a statement of trust, declaring that the purchase has been made on behalf of the fund. The solicitor handling your contract can arrange for the statement to be drawn up.

A variation to the statement of trust is to have minutes drafted approving and confirming the purchase has been made for the SMSF. These minutes will need to be presented at a trustee meeting.

Should you forget the name of your fund trustee and you happen to be purchasing property either at an auction or private sale my recommendation would be to include the words 'or nominee' in addition to your name as the name of the purchaser on the contract note. This allows you to provide the correct name later (but I would take legal advice on this to make sure).

Now, you're probably thinking, who could possibly forget their fund trustee's name? Believe you me, it happens more often than you think. I've had people purchasing property as individual trustees, despite the fact that the SMSF has a corporate trustee. I've had husbands forgetting their wives were trustees, parents who've ignored the fact that a child or children were members of the fund and people providing the name of the family trust trustee instead of the SMSF trustee!

In most instances these inaccuracies were rectified prior to the purchase being finalised.

However, should this not be picked up and the title is issued in the wrong name, you will incur solicitor's fees to fix the problem and you will also have to pay a fee to the Titles Office.

Note: When paying a deposit on the property, this can be paid with a cheque from your fund, your business or from your personal account. If payment comes from the second or third options, it may be treated as part of your fund contributions for that financial year.

Alternatively, provided the deposit doesn't exceed 10 per cent of your fund's value, it can be treated as a short-term loan to your fund. However, this must be paid back within seven days.

Key Points

- Additional contributions into your SMSF to allow affordability of property purchases must not exceed the contribution caps.

- You can make *in specie* contributions comprising 'business real property' into your SMSF.

- Buying off the plan can offer an SMSF leverage. You should always apply caution when buying off the plan through your SMSF as legislation can change.

CHAPTER 8

Borrowing to invest

PROBABLY THE reason you bought this book is because you are considering borrowing to buy property through an SMSF. This has now been an option since September 2007 and as we have discussed it is becoming a popular way of diversifying your investments and using leverage in an attempt to fast-track growth.

Self managed super funds are now able to purchase anything they could previously acquire with cash – such as property, Australian and overseas shares, managed funds, private equity investments, even collectables – with borrowings, as long as it is a 'single' asset or collection of identical assets. This places some restrictions on sharemarket investors who are fine to take a loan via their self managed super fund to buy say, 1,000 BHP-Billiton shares but if they want to buy 1,000 BHP-Billiton plus 1,000 Commonwealth Bank shares they would have to set up two gearing structures. Costs involved with this could make it an unattractive option. This book is concerned predominantly with property investing and property investors usually buy one property at a time, so no such conditions will phase them.

Differences between investing through an SMSF and in your own name

Before I get down to the nitty gritty of borrowing to invest in property, let's take a quick look at three differences between an individual buying property with borrowings and an SMSF doing the same thing. Remember, just because you *can* do something doesn't necessarily mean you *should*.

The first difference is related to security for the loan. When an individual purchases property with borrowings – be it residential or commercial property – the lender requires the property as security for the loan and often demands additional property as security. When an SMSF purchases a property with borrowings, the only property that can be used as security is the property acquired.

The second difference is in the financing of the loan. As a result of further Commonwealth government changes to SMSF borrowing rules, key issues have been clarified, one being that funds can only refinance loans if a better deal is found. But if the loan is refinanced, it can only be for the existing debt plus the costs of refinancing.

Thirdly, and very importantly, SMSF trustees are required to seek advice from a licensed adviser before they can go ahead and borrow through their SMSF. The Government has advised on more than one occasion its intention to make this a legal requirement. At the time of writing, it can be a requirement of lenders such as banks.

Borrowing to buy – the step-by-step process

As there is a little more involved when you borrow to buy property through your SMSF, I thought I would break it down into easy-to-follow steps.

1. Discuss your intention to buy a property by borrowing with your SMSF adviser.
2. Establish a security or 'bare' trust.
3. Find a suitable property to purchase.
4. Enter into a contract to purchase the property.
5. Sign an agreement to transfer.
6. Pay the deposit.
7. Take out a limited recourse loan.
8. Manage the property.
9. Transfer title to the SMSF.

We will look at each step in turn.

Seeking professional advice

Before even starting to look for property it is advisable to comply with this part of the legislation and talk to a professional adviser with expertise in the area of SMSF management and legislation. If the adviser agrees that the proposed level of borrowing and the intended property meet the regulatory requirements, then he or she must provide you (and the fund) with written advice to this effect. You may find a property before getting professional advice under circumstances such as those outlined in the example below.

Example

Chris and Fiona attend an auction of a residential property. They are the successful bidders and complete a contract note which indicates the buyer as Chris and Fiona or a nominee. The vendor was a complete stranger so the transaction would meet the arm's length requirement.

Next Chris and Fiona contact their accountant to ask for advice as to who the buyer should be. The options available are to buy the property in one of their names, both of their names, in the name of their family trust or their SMSF. Borrowing will be required in all cases to finance the purchase. Having considered the alternatives, their accountant contacts Matt, a financial planner licensed to advise on SMSF borrowings.

Matt reviews Chris and Fiona's situation and on satisfying himself that it is appropriate, recommends they purchase the property via their self managed super fund.

Establishing a security trust

When an individual buys a property, the parties involved in the transaction are the vendor, the buyer and the lender. However, when borrowings are used to purchase property through an SMSF, the buyer splits into two:

- the SMSF; and
- the security trust.

As we have already stated, when an SMSF borrows to acquire property, the lender automatically requires the property as security for the debt. However, superannuation funds are not in the position at law to pledge an asset as security for a loan. To get round this problem, the property is held in a separate entity, commonly called a 'security' or 'bare' trust. The sole beneficiary of the security trust is the superannuation fund. The sole purpose of a security trust is to be the 'interim' owner of the property until the loan has been repaid in full. After that, ownership reverts to the SMSF.

Your adviser can arrange to have a 'security' trust set up for you in much the same way as he or she would have a discretionary trust created.

It is important to keep in mind that a security trust can only hold ONE property or asset at a time. Should the SMSF decide to purchase more properties with borrowings, these will have their own security trusts. However, once the debt has been repaid and ownership of the property is transferred to the SMSF trustee, the security trust can be used again to purchase another property with borrowings.

Each security trust must also have a trustee. Ideally this should not be the SMSF trustee but it can be a company owned by members of the fund (with one or more members as shareholders and directors) or the trustee can be a professional trustee company. The majority of people are electing to have a company they own as trustee.

I am finding that lenders are increasingly requesting that trustees of the security trust be separate trustees to the SMSF trustee.

The security trust trustee can be trustee of more than one security trust at any given time.

Because the security trust is only holding the property and not undertaking any operational activities, it does not have to prepare accounts and/or lodge a tax return each year. Rental income is paid to the SMSF which is liable for repaying the loan and paying expenses not covered by the tenant.

Finding the right property

Any detail on this next step is really beyond the scope of this book. There are plenty of books on the market that will help you with property selection. Suffice to say here that you make a considered purchase bearing in mind the income and capital gain this purchase will contribute to your SMSF and the costs involved with making the purchase and managing the property. There are buyers' agents who will source suitable property for you. Or simply find a good real estate agent.

Entering the contract

Upon purchase, the title of the property must be in the name of the trustee of the security trust. Although, when the loan has been repaid in full and ownership returns to the SMSF, the title will be transferred into the name of the SMSF trustee. Registration of ownership of a property differs between the states and territories. In some states only the name of the trustee of the security/bare trust will be shown. I would suggest the trustee in these states make a statement of trust confirming it is holding the property in its capacity as trustee of the security or bare trust.

The transfer agreement

Fundamental to SMSFs being able to borrow to invest is the transfer agreement. This is a legal agreement that gives a person, in this case the SMSF trustee, the right to acquire a property but not until a pre-determined 'condition' has been met. In this instance, the condition is that the debt on the property is repaid in full before the fund takes ownership. Changes to legislation now require the transfer of ownership to take effect upon final payment of the debt. The super-annuation fund could be in breach of superannuation legislation if this is delayed. Your solicitor will prepare the transfer agreement to be signed by the trustee.

Paying the deposit

Lenders loaning money to an SMSF tend to ask for much larger deposits than individual investors or home-buyers would normally be used to. Deposits can range from 20 per cent to 50 per cent of the property's value. The fund also has to pay stamp duty and any other costs such as conveyancing, and costs associated with establishing the agreement to transfer and the security trust and initial advice.

These larger deposits are there to protect all parties because the only security for the loan is the property itself.

The size of the deposit also depends on:

- **The type of property being acquired.** Loans for residential property may attract a deposit of up to 30 per cent, for commercial property up to 35 per cent and rural property (for farm purchases) 50 per cent. All loans are subject to a valuation which is ordered and instructed by the lender.

- **Location of the property.** A property may be deemed greater risk to a lender if it is a specialised property, for example premises that have been designed for a specific industry or business, or if it is in an area where it may be more difficult to sell, i.e. in a remote or rural area.

- **The lender's own internal rules.** These may require a different deposit to that shown above.

The deposit can be paid using other funds in the SMSF or a member can pay the deposit with money held outside of the fund as a contribution (be careful in doing so not to exceed those caps).

Taking out a limited recourse loan

In order to protect other assets in the SMSF, legislation will only allow the use of a 'limited recourse' loan.

Unlike a traditional mortgage, where a lender can repossess, sell the property and still demand repayment of any remaining outstanding amount from the borrower, a limited recourse loan limits the lender's recovery to the property only, leaving other assets in the super fund intact.

This means that the only security available to the lender is the property being acquired and in the event of a default, the only security the lender has is the property in the security trust. A lender can, however, request the SMSF members give a personal guarantee.

The fees involved in setting up loans vary from lender to lender. Typically there is an establishment fee. However, lenders may also impose risk fees, loan service fees and could also have exit fees, title insurance fees, completion fees, right to repay fees, legal fees and so on. My recommendation would be to compare carefully different lenders to establish what your overall costs will be. Alternatively, engage a good mortgage broker and he or she will investigate the options available. Let's have a look at an example.

Example:

Tenzing has established his own SMSF and rolled over his member balance from the fund into which his employer had previously been contributing. Having followed the steps above, he is now ready to obtain the loan required to acquire the chosen property. Tenzing seeks out the assistance of Assunta, a mortgage broker, who provides him with details of the various loans available to him and their costs both establishment and ongoing.

Interest rates on loans to super funds are now more or less the same as rates for individual property investors.

It is important to remember that loan repayments and other expenses come from the super fund, not the security trust. Likewise when the property is rented out, all rental income will go to the fund.

The terms of a limited recourse loan are negotiable and are available for the same periods as loans made to individuals purchasing outside their superannuation fund. The term chosen can be based on the amount of cash in the fund available as a deposit, as well as future cash flow, with cash flow determining the level of repayments. The higher the deposit and the greater the amount available for repayments, the shorter the number of years required to repay the loan.

Ultimately, there is little or no benefit to be had from having debt inside super so paying off a loan as quickly as possible frees you up to make further investments.

You can elect to take out a principal and interest loan or an interest-only loan. With the latter, the loan would either be repaid from the fund's accumulated contributions and earnings or on the sale of the property.

While many investors are used to the idea of negative gearing when they invest in property personally, it is not as beneficial when an SMSF is buying the property as an SMSF only pays tax at the rate of 15 per cent. If someone on the top marginal tax rate negatively gears an investment outside of super and makes a loss of $1,000, this will reduce his or her income tax by $465 (being 46.5 per cent – the top marginal rate – of $1,000). For an SMSF the tax saving is only $150. So negative gearing offers very little benefit.

Borrowing from related parties, such as a fund member, your family trust or a company you own is allowed under legislation governing superannuation funds. Sometimes this occurs because the member has arranged to borrow personally and then he or she on-loans some or all of this money to the SMSF. If this is the situation, then the interest rate for the loan to the SMSF should be no less than the rate at which the individual has borrowed. However, if you have the spare funds, perhaps from an inheritance, there are less restrictions on the interest rate you would charge on a loan made to your SMSF.

Renting out the property

When it comes to renting out investment property, there are differences associated with renting out property purchased for cash and property acquired with borrowings.

To better explain how the process works, I will initially take a look at what happens when the SMSF purchases the property with cash.

In this scenario, the SMSF trustee owns the property. When rented out, the tenant pays rent to the SMSF.

Example:

Serhan's SMSF buys a shop which it rents to Kendra, a hairdresser who uses the shop to operate her business from. The tenant, being Kendra's business, pays rent to the trustee of Serhan's superannuation fund.

The following diagram illustrates this:

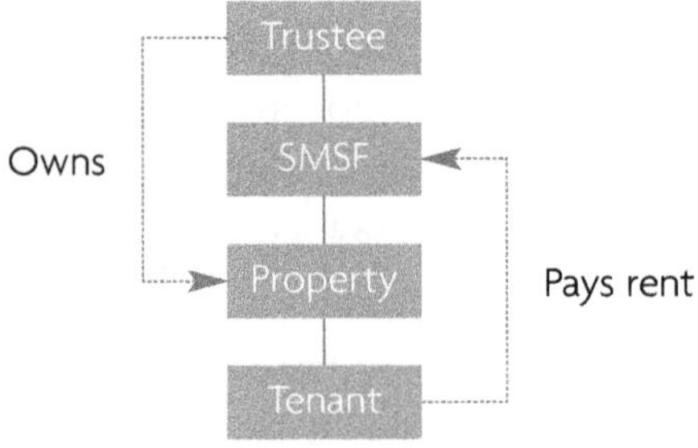

Example (cont'd)

However, when the property is purchased with borrowings, although the title to the property is held by the security trust and stands as security for the borrowings, the tenant pays rent to the trustee of the superannuation fund (see diagram below).

The SMSF trustee is also responsible for paying the interest on the loan.

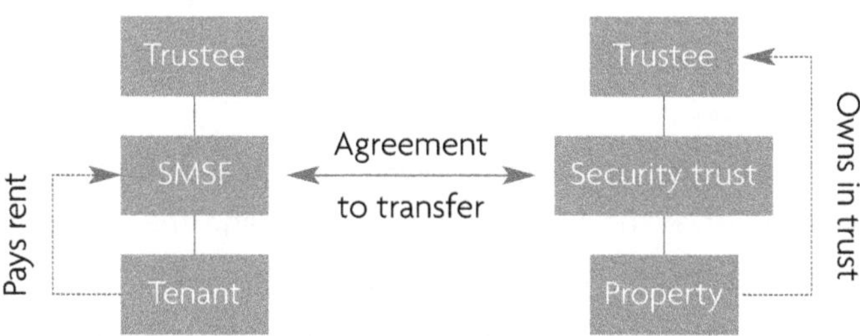

From Kendra's perspective and that of her business, there is no difference – rent simply continues to be paid to Serhan's SMSF.

It is worth pointing out that if the loan was a principal and interest loan, as it is repaid the SMSF's interest in the property increases.

Transferring title to the SMSF

Once the debt is paid in full, the SMSF trustee asks the trustee of the security trust to transfer ownership of the property to the fund.

Very importantly, because of legislative changes in 2010, if ownership of the property is not transferred once the debt has been repaid the SMSF may find itself in breach of legislation governing superannuation funds.

When the property is transferred from the security trust to the SMSF, there may be some stamp duty, albeit nominal, that may be required in some states and territories.

Taking Chris and Fiona as an example, let's take a look at what typically happens during the life of the loan.

Example:

Although the trustee of their SMSF is CF Super Pty Ltd (a company they are both directors of), they have named their security trust trustee, CF Security Pty Ltd. Both are directors.

Chris and Fiona will at all times control their SMSF and their security trust.

Initially the property will be owned by CF Security Pty Ltd. However, once the loan has been repaid and the mortgage discharged, ownership will be transferred to CF Super Pty Ltd.

Very importantly this transfer will not result in a capital gains tax (CGT) event. However, nominal stamp duty may be payable in some states. Also, because the relevant Titles Office views this as a change of ownership, Chris and Fiona can expect to incur a small fee.

If the property were to be sold prior to the debt being repaid, the proceeds would first be used to pay out the balance of the mortgage with the remaining money going to the SMSF. In this instance it would be considered a CGT event and tax would be paid on any profit made.

Because Chris and Fiona's fund had held on to the property for more than 12 months, they will be entitled to a one-third discount on the profit made before calculating CGT (see Chapter 9 on CGT). They will pay 15 per cent in tax if the fund is in accumulation mode but if both are retired and receiving a pension or income stream, the rate reduces to zero.

The security trust and/or its trustee could be wound up when the property is sold or should Chris and Fiona want to buy another property with borrowings, they could use this same trust.

The pros and cons of borrowing to buy

To round off the discussion on borrowing through your SMSF to buy property, I've summarised the pros and cons. First, the upside of using borrowings to purchase property are:

- You can acquire a property immediately even though you don't have the cash to pay for it in full, enabling you to enjoy the benefits of capital appreciation without having to wait. Depending on location and the type of property, the past few years have seen a considerable appreciation in some property values.

- It allows diversification of investments. By way of example, a couple with a super balance of $500,000, could invest $250,000 in a property, borrowing the balance of the price of the property, and invest the remaining $250,000 in the sharemarket and/or fixed interest.

The downside of borrowing through your SMSF:

- Outgoings on the property (interest on the loan plus property expenses) could be greater than rental income, particularly if you have problems with tenants and subsequent high vacancy rates.

- If you opt for a principal and interest loan, you are committed to making regular loan repayments. This may mean additional contributions have to be made to the superannuation fund at a time when it is not convenient. This could occur, for example, if either the property ceased to be tenanted or the tenant failed to pay the required rent.

- There are additional costs involved with acquiring a property with borrowings. Although these will vary depending on who assists with establishing the structures and preparing the documentation, there will be a cost and it may not be viable for a low value property.

Keys Points

- SMSFs are now allowed to use borrowings to invest in property, shares and other assets.
- A 'security' or 'bare trust' holds the property in trust until the SMSF has paid off the loan, and then the SMSF takes ownership of the property from the security trust.
- Legislation only allows the SMSF to take out a 'limited recourse loan'.

CHAPTER 9

How your property investment is taxed

SOMEONE ONCE said that there are only two certainties in life – death and taxes. Avoiding the topic of death until we discuss succession planning in Chapter 13, let's now consider taxes.

Most people don't mind paying taxes. After all, they fund roads and schools and hospitals as well as a whole range of other essential services. However, no one likes paying too much tax and it is acceptable to consider ways to minimise the tax you pay.

One of the attractions of investing through superannuation is that it's concessionally-taxed.

Property is an attractive investment because it generates income in the form of rents from tenants and also, if you invest wisely, a capital gain as the property increases in value over the years. Purchasing property via a self managed super fund allows you to access significant tax concessions on rental income and capital gains on the profit when the property is sold.

Let's look at each in turn.

Taxation of rental income

How income is taxed in a super fund depends on in what phase the fund is in its life-cycle. (The life-cycle of a fund was discussed in detail in Chapter 3.) If the fund is in its accumulation stage (i.e. the members are still contributing over their working lives) then all income earned by the SMSF, provided the fund complies with super legislation, is taxed at the concessional rate of 15 per cent. So any rental income from a property purchased through your SMSF – either directly or with borrowings – is taxed at 15 per cent during the accumulation stage.

When members start to draw on their SMSF for an income in retirement, the fund's earnings are not taxed at all. Also, provided the members are aged 60 or more, they pay no tax on money they receive from the fund.

If the fund is transitioning from the accumulation to the retirement stage, and a transition to retirement income stream (TRIS) is being paid to members aged over preservation age, (currently 55 years but rising to age 60 by 2024), then part of the SMSF's income will still be taxed at 15 per cent. The balance may then be subject to a 0 per cent tax rate. Your accountant or superannuation administrator can advise you in more detail on your particular circumstances.

Income may be offset by allowable deductions for any expenses incurred in earning this income in your SMSF, just as it would were the income being earned by an individual or a company or a trust. What is assessable or deductible for one form of ownership is the same for the other.

When your SMSF owns property, it will either have to pay tax on the net income or use a loss to offset tax on other income.

Capital gains tax (GCT)

For the majority of us, the main reason for investing in property is to make a profit on the eventual sale. When you sell your family home there is no capital gains tax payable on any profits you have made. However, with all other investments you will pay capital gains tax on at least part of the profits realised when you sell it. If you sell a property within twelve months of the date of purchase you will pay capital gains tax on the total profit from the sale.

The majority of property owners invest for longer than 12 months and so they will qualify for the CGT discounts. An individual is entitled to an exemption (or discount) on 50 per cent of the realised gain from the sale of an investment property. Where a property is owned by a trust (a unit trust or discretionary trust), beneficiaries will also be entitled to a 50 per cent tax exemption on their share of the profit. If the property is owned by your SMSF, assuming that one or more members are under 'preservation age' (currently 55), profits will qualify for a one-third CGT discount.

At face value, then, isn't it better to invest in property outside of your SMSF?

No it isn't. While buying personally entitles you to an exemption on 50 per cent of the gain, you will still have to pay tax at your marginal rate on the other 50 per cent – and for taxpayers in the top margin bracket this means paying tax at a rate of 46.5 per cent (including the Medicare levy). Self managed super funds, however, will only have to pay 15 per cent tax on two-thirds of the profit.

Let me use an example to better explain.

Example

Tim and Angela have purchased property in their own names. They hold on to it for several years before selling it for $420,000 (after deducting expenses such as agents' fees). This gives them a profit of $100,000.

Assuming the property was owned equally between them, this would give them a capital gain of $50,000 each.

Once the 50 per cent tax exemption has been applied, the remaining $25,000 will be subject to tax. Let's assume this amount, when added to other income, leaves them in the 32.5 per cent tax bracket. This means their total tax bill from the sale of the property (including their Medicare levy) will come to $17,000 (34% of $25,000 for both Tim and Angela).

Unfortunately, the greater the realised gain, when added to other income, the greater the potential to slip into a higher tax bracket. For instance, if they were in the 37 per cent tax bracket, the tax plus Medicare levy payable would increase to $19,250.

However, had Tim and Angela's SMSF purchased the property, $33,333 of the profit would be exempt from tax, with the remaining $66,667 taxed at 15 per cent, giving them a total tax bill of $10,000.

This is a saving of $7,000 and potentially more when compared to investing personally.

If Tim and Angela had retired and commenced an income stream or pension from their SMSF prior to selling the property, there would be no tax payable on the property, giving them an even larger net profit – $100,000 compared to $83,000 ($100,000 gain less $17,000 personal tax) for an investment that cost them just $320,000.

We will make more comparisons between owning property personally and through an SMSF in the next chapter.

Taxation at preservation age

When SMSF superannuants reach preservation age (currently 55), they can continue making contributions to their fund despite having commenced a Transition to Retirement Income Stream (TRIS). (A TRIS is a form of pension discussed in Chapter 3 that SMSFs can pay to members aged 55 to 64 even if they are still working.) Basically, they are considered to be members twice over – first as pensioners and secondly as members in accumulation mode.

When members begin receiving a TRIS, this has a significant impact on the tax rate applicable to any capital gains. At this time, SMSF trustees can decide to 'segregate' the assets of the fund. This means they nominate which assets are to be used to provide a pension or income stream. These are segregated in the 'income stream' account. The remaining assets – or non income stream assets – are held in the 'accumulation' account.

Alternatively, trustees can decide against separating assets into pension and accumulation accounts and instead rely on an annual actuarial certificate to specify the percentage of the fund's income that belongs to each type of account.

Either way, income and capital gains arising from investments in the accumulation account would be taxed at 15 per cent and investments in TRIS/pension accounts would incur no tax.

This may appear complex and periodically it is. I would suggest you talk with your accountant or superannuation adviser to determine whether to 'segregate' funds or gain actuarial advice.

So what does all this mean when it comes to property?

Depending on the value of the property and the amount

held in the fund for pensioner members, the trustees may decide that the property will form part of the fund's pension assets. If this occurs, the realised gain will be tax exempt when the property is sold.

Let's take a look at how this works in practice.

Example

Mark is 60 and has his own SMSF. He has $800,000 in his 'income stream' account. His SMSF owns a property valued at $600,000. If this property formed part of the assets providing his pension, there would be no CGT on the sale of the property.

Alternatively, if Mark's TRIS account is valued at $300,000, then the maximum amount of the property that could be considered part of the 'income stream' or 'pension' assets would be $300,000.

In this scenario, if the property was sold, only half of the gain would be tax exempt and the other half taxable.

Let's assume the property had been purchased by the fund for $400,000 more than twelve months ago. Then, as the property is allocated equally between his accumulation and pension accounts, the tax payable on the $200,000 capital gain when the property is sold would be calculated as:

- Pension account – $100,000 gain, no tax.
- Accumulation account – $100,000 less one-third discount of $33,333, tax payable at the rate of 15 per cent of the balance with an amount of $10,000 to be paid.

As the example shows, if the property cannot be fully allocated to the pension account, then part of the gain will be taxable at 15 per cent and the rest is tax free. Alternatively, if Mark was retired and using all of his account balance to provide a pension, then 100 per cent of the realised gain would be tax free.

When do we sell?

The 15 per cent tax payable on the discounted capital gain applies when all members in the SMSF are in accumulation mode – typically under preservation age (currently 55 years) at the time of the sale. However, it drops to zero when all fund members are retired and receiving a pension or income stream from the fund.

So, not surprisingly, for those approaching retirement (or preservation age) there is an enormous incentive to delay selling property until the fund is in the retirement stage of its life-cycle.

One question frequently asked by SMSF trustees is, "How long after retiring and starting a pension do we have to wait before selling property?"

And the answer is that there is no minimum period. You could, if you like, sell the day after your income stream commences.

It's not unknown for SMSF trustees to delay selling a property until after income streams have commenced.

Negative gearing

We touched upon negative gearing briefly in the previous chapter. It is a common strategy used by high income earners to save money on tax and benefit from capital appreciation of property. Basically, the way it works is investors buy a property and the rental income it generates is LESS than the outgoings (e.g. loan repayments, ongoing management and maintenance costs). This loss is offset against other taxable income.

Simplistically, this strategy is not suited to SMSF investment because the amount of tax on income would only 15 per cent or less anyway. Let's look at an example.

Example

In the first half of 2010 I met with Tim and Angela who we referred to in an earlier example. They were looking to buy property in regional Victoria. The property was going to cost them $320,000 and was expected to generate a net rental income of around $7,000 per annum. They had the cash to pay for the property and could either buy it personally or deposit the money in their SMSF and buy it as a superannuation investment.

If they acquired the property personally, the income tax and Medicare levy on the net rental each year would be $2,380 (that is, 34 per cent of $7,000). This is because both Tim and Angela are expecting a personal income of between $37,000 and $80,000 for each year of ownership. If either or both exceeded $80,000, then a higher tax rate would apply.

However, if they bought the property through their SMSF their tax would drop to $1,050 (15 per cent of $7,000) – a dramatic saving indeed! And better still – when Tim and Angela retire or begin drawing an income stream, their SMSF will no longer pay tax on the $7,000 rental income each year.

If however, **borrowings** were required to assist in purchasing the property, then the year by year outcome would be different.

Example (cont'd)

For the purposes of this example let's assume a loan was required for part of the property purchase and that the interest was $8,000 a year.

A loss would be made irrespective of whether they owned the property personally or with their fund. Offsetting this loss against other income would save Tim and Angela $340 each year in income tax and Medicare levy if they owned the property in their own names. If the property was purchased through the SMSF it would only save $150 in income tax.

When making the decision to acquire the property, and assuming they were going to borrow in order to purchase, Tim and Angela would have to consider the annual tax savings if the property was negatively geared against the estimated capital gains tax when the property was eventually sold.

They know the fund has a maximum rate of 15 per cent and it could be as low as zero, whereas the amount of realised gain could move Angela and Tim into a higher tax bracket if the property was owned personally. If they stayed in the same personal tax bracket, the tax rate on the capital gain would be 34 per cent.

Key Points

- SMSFs pay between 0 per cent and 15 per cent tax on the fund's income, depending on the phase the fund is in.

- Capital gains tax is discounted by one-third and then taxed at 15 per cent within the super fund.

- Negative gearing is generally not an attractive investment strategy for SMSFs.

CHAPTER 10

SMSF versus personal property ownership

THERE HAS been a worrying increase in the number of property developers and property promoters encouraging potential property investors to purchase with their superannuation money. In some cases, they even offer to set up an SMSF on your behalf. These promoters are not being kind or helpful, they are just trying to find new markets to sell their property – often at inflated prices.

There is undoubtedly growing interest in purchasing property with self managed super funds since the option of borrowing to invest became a possibility but this approach is not necessarily always the best way to go. Under some circumstances buying in your own name could be a much better choice.

My advice to those of you unsure which path to choose is to take a good hard look at how you are likely to benefit and allow this to determine the choices you make.

The key factors to consider when you are weighing up whether to invest in property through an SMSF or as an individual are:

- How your investment will be taxed.
- The income and expenditure associated with the purchase and ongoing management of the property.
- How you will repay the debt.

We look at each in turn and I will provide some examples to better illustrate these points.

How your investment will be taxed

For the majority of people, the differences in tax treatment will determine how they purchase their property. We discussed taxation in the previous chapter but will look at it again now for comparative purposes.

Capital gains tax

The key difference between owning property personally and through an SMSF is the amount of CGT you will pay on the realised gain when the property is sold or 'disposed' of. Disposal could include transferring the property to fund members to live in when they retire.

If the property has been retained for more than twelve months (in practice, a minimum of twelve months and two days), irrespective of whether the property is owned personally or by the fund, the realised gain will be 'discounted' or reduced before CGT is calculated.

If you own the property personally, there will be a 50 per cent discount – that is, the profit will be discounted by 50 per cent before tax is calculated. If the property is owned by your SMSF, the realised gain will be discounted by one-third.

Capital gains tax on a personal investment is calculated at the individual's marginal tax rate. The discounted gain from the sale of property is added to other income and could have the effect of pushing the investor from a tax rate of 34 per cent for people on incomes in the $37,001 to $80,000 range into a much higher tax bracket – either 38.5 per cent or 46.5 per cent, depending on the level of gain.

Tax would then be applied at marginal rates (34 per cent, 38.5 per cent and 46.5 per cent including the Medicare levy) depending on the individual's circumstances. For many people part of the gain would be taxed at one rate and the balance at another. The outcome would be a significantly higher amount.

As we noted in the previous chapter, the discounted capital gain will be taxed at 15 per cent or 0 per cent if the property had been acquired through an SMSF.

Income and expenditure from investment

Another key determinant of whether to purchase property personally or via an SMSF, is the amount of income generated by the investment and the expenses associated with it.

If the intention is to negatively gear the investment and use the annual loss to offset income tax on other income, owning the property personally provides a much better outcome, as we saw in the example in the previous chapter. In this situation, because the SMSF only pays tax at 15 per cent, any loss as a result of negative gearing only has a 15 per cent tax benefit.

However, because personal property investors typically have marginal tax rates of 34 per cent, 38.5 per cent and 46.5 per cent (including the Medicare levy), any loss will have a significantly higher tax benefit if they invest outside super.

If the property is expected to have little or no capital gain in the period that you intend to hold it, then there may be greater tax benefits if it is held personally.

If your aim is to eliminate debt, or at least reduce it to a level where the property will be neutrally geared, then there will be no annual loss to offset against other income, reducing the advantage of a personal investment over an SMSF investment.

My experience has been that the majority of self managed funds want to eliminate the debt as quickly as possible. In some circumstances this is because trustees want full owner- ship of the property, while on other occasions it is about repaying debt in order to acquire a second, or even a third property.

Debt repayment

The third factor which determines how to purchase property is debt repayment. Will buying via your SMSF enable you to discharge your debt quicker than buying in your own name or vice versa?

One of the key advantages of your SMSF buying property is the opportunity to speed up capital repayments on the loan by increasing the amount of concessional (pre-tax) contribu- tions going into the fund.

These contributions are made by self-employed individuals and employers who are required to contribute, from July 2013, 9.25 per cent of employees' salaries into super – a figure that will increase to 12 per cent over the next few years. These contributions are taxed at 15 per cent at the time they go into the fund and are tax-deductible to individuals or companies making the contribution. There are restrictions in the form of contribution caps which we discussed in Chapter 2.

Keeping in mind the contribution caps, how can SMSF

superannuants bump up their concessional contributions to repay debt faster?

Let's look at an example to explain how.

Example

Sarika earns $60,000 per year. Her employer is required to contribute $5,550 (9.25 per cent of $60,000) into her super. Sarika could arrange for her employer to reduce her salary by $5,000 and pay this into her fund as well. To gauge the effectiveness of this strategy:

- had Sarika received the $5,000 as salary, she would have to pay $1,700 in the form of tax and the Medicare levy (34 per cent of $5,000)
- instead, by salary sacrificing the $5,000 in her SMSF, she only has $750 to pay in tax (15 per cent of $5,000).

By salary sacrificing, Sarika has gained an additional $950 that can be used for repaying her debt on the property. This amount is the difference between the tax she would have paid personally and the tax paid by her superannuation fund.

As a result of the compulsory contribution of $5,550 and the salary sacrifice amount of $5,000, Sarika has a net after tax amount of $8,967.50 ($5,550 + $5,000 less 15 per cent tax) available to assist with repaying the debt on the property.

People who buy property in their own name or via an entity such as their family trust will have to make principal repayments on the loan using after tax-money before any repayments have been made.

This partly explains why investors buying property in their own names often prefer using interest-only loans. In such cases the debt is only repaid when the property is sold. Naturally, this can lead to increased interest.

So how do you choose?

When making a decision about how you will purchase, it is worth giving consideration to the following questions:

- Why are you investing? Is it for the expected capital gain or to reduce your current level of income tax?
- What amount of capital gain do you expect to receive? Remember, the greater the gain, the lower the preferred tax rate.
- What access to the money do you want when the property is sold? If you own the property personally, you will always have access. If it is owned by the SMSF, the money must remain inside the super fund until you at least reach preservation age.
- What tax do you want to pay in retirement?

Below I have provided two examples. One is an illustration of when buying personally with cash is the best option and the other of when purchasing via an SMSF with borrowings has the best possible outcome.

However, before looking at these, here's a quick recap.

One advantage of buying property personally is the opportunity to negatively gear the investment and offset the annual loss against other income. The advantage of investing through an SMSF is the lower tax rate on capital gains (15 per cent if you have not reached preservation age and zero if you have retired and are receiving a pension or income stream from your SMSF or you can allocate the property wholly to a transition to retirement income stream (TRIS) account).

Also, keep in mind that the costs of acquiring property will impact on the amount of CGT payable when the property is sold. This is because expenses, such as stamp duty, can be added to the cost base for the CGT calculation. Because these costs vary between states and territories, I am going to ignore them for the purposes of this comparison.

We will look at two purchasers: Linda who decides to buy the property via her fund and Sarah who opts to buy hers personally. With both we will look at the impact of these investment choices using cash and buying with debt. These examples will focus on buying property with the intention of making a capital gain when sold. It is very important to note that the assumptions used can have a significant effect on the outcome.

Irrespective of what property is acquired, there will be a profit each year in that rental income will almost always be greater than property expenses. This assumes, of course, that the property will always be fully tenanted and there is no major maintenance.

Example 1: Buying with cash as an individual and through an SMSF

Linda and Sarah both receive an inheritance of $450,000. Being under the age of 65 and not having exceeded the superannuation contribution caps in the previous two tax years, Linda puts her inheritance into her SMSF. Sarah does not.

Linda has another $50,000 in cash in her fund. Sarah also has an additional $50,000 in cash which she adds to her inheritance. Both buy a property for $500,000 and decide to hold it for a 10-year period.

While Linda's SMSF pays tax at the rate of 15 per cent on the net income from the property (the rent) over the next 10 years, Sarah pays tax at marginal tax rates on the net income. Over the 10 year period, the properties increase in value at, say, 4 per cent per annum. This is just 1 per cent above the Reserve Bank's upper-end target range for inflation.

Ten years on, the properties are worth $740,120. Both women decide to sell. To simplify, let's ignore the costs incurred in selling the properties. Both women make a profit of $240,120 ($740,120 − $500,000).

What is the CGT on each property?

Because they have been held for longer than 12 months, Linda and Sarah are each entitled to receive some of their capital gain tax-free.

Given that Sarah owned the property personally, she is only required to pay tax on 50 per cent of the gain − $120,060. This is payable at marginal tax rates. Clearly, her income for the year in which the sale occurs will be above the level at which the 32.5 per cent marginal rate changes to 37 per cent. Whether this increase takes her into the 45 per cent category is very dependent on other income. The Medicare levy is added to these rates.

If we assume Sarah's other income is $60,000 with a marginal tax rate of 32.5 per cent, the gain of $120,060 will lift her just into the 45 per cent tax bracket. As a result of the property sale, she will pay tax of $45,328 ($20,000 @ 34 per cent, $100,000 @ 37.5 per cent and $60 @ 46.5 per cent, allowing for the Medicare levy) on the capital gain. This is in addition to the tax payable on the $60,000 income.

Linda's SMSF is entitled to a one-third discount on the profit for tax purposes, meaning its taxable income will be $160,080.

Because superannuation funds pay tax at the rate of 15 per cent, Linda's SMSF tax bill will be $24,012 (15 per cent of $160,080). This is $21,316 less than Sarah or expressed another way, an additional 4.26 per cent profit on the original investment amount.

If, prior to the sale taking place, Linda had retired and started a pension, the tax bill would be even less. The tax rate on the fund's income would be reduced to zero, which means the profit will not be taxed, giving her an additional $45,328 (or an extra 9 per cent profit.)

However, once costs associated with buying and selling the property are taken into account, the difference between the two outcomes becomes a little less. The higher the costs incurred, the less tax that will be payable.

In summary, Linda will pay less tax on the annual net income and significantly less tax on the realised capital gains.

Example 2: Borrowing to buy property as an individual and through an SMSF

Rather than put all of their money into the one investment, Linda and Sarah decide to diversify, or spread the money, between different investments. They may even use some of their inheritances to pay off some non-tax deductible debt such as credit cards.

Let's assume they buy a $500,000 residential property and put down $150,000 as a deposit and borrow the remaining $350,000.

Some investors prefer interest-only loans while others prefer paying off the principal. For the purposes of this example we assume they will use a principal and interest loan. In this situation, irrespective of the type of loan Linda and Sarah choose to use, if the rental income from the property is less than the expenses associated with the property (such as loan interest and rates), Sarah will benefit most year on year.

This is because Sarah (who is investing personally), under current tax law can offset her yearly loss against other income that would be taxable at her marginal rate – be it 34 per cent, 38.5 per cent or 46.5 per cent.

While Linda's SMSF can offset the loss against other income it receives, the tax rate for her fund is only 15 per cent.

If your primary intention when investing in property is to reduce tax on other income as a result of negative gearing, then, clearly, owning the property personally is the better option. Conversely, if the property is to be positively geared (i.e. the income is greater than expenses) it is preferable for the property to be owned by the SMSF.

However, as we saw above there are significant differences when CGT is considered.

There is another big difference between investing in your own name and your SMSF. And this concerns principal repayments on the loan. A member of a superannuation fund can obtain a tax deduction on some/all of the principal repayments made in any year.

How does this occur? Simply, an employer or a self-employed person can make superannuation contributions up to $25,000 per annum ($35,000 from July 2013 if the person is aged 59 or more). The payer receives a tax deduction of 30 per cent if a company contributes or the marginal tax rate if a self-employed person makes the payment. The superannuation fund pays tax at the rate of 15 per cent.

The result is an immediate profit – the difference between the tax deduction and the tax payable. If you operate your own business you determine the amount you contribute. If you are employed, check with your employer about making salary sacrifice contributions.

From the employer's perspective, there is no fringe benefit tax (FBT) payable and salary sacrifice contributions won't affect either payroll tax or workers compensation premiums.

Back to the example. I have assumed both Linda and Sarah purchase their properties using principal and interest loans. Because there are differences between borrowing personally and borrowing via a superannuation fund, the lenders require higher deposits for SMSF borrowings and may apply a slightly higher interest rate.

As an illustration of this difference, I asked two of our larger banks for a quote for this example. In October 2013, there was a 0.85 per cent difference for a 25 year principal and interest loan. In practice, with a loan of $350,000, after allowing for the differing ongoing fees, the difference in repayments was slightly less than $190 per month.

Sarah will make principal repayments with after-tax dollars. Although Linda could salary sacrifice and increase her contributions, I have assumed for the purposes of this example she makes personal contributions having paid tax.

This removes the impact of personal tax benefits which both can obtain and focuses on the principal reason many people invest in property – the capital gain.

Interest rates will fluctuate over time and our assumption is this will affect the overall outcome. Let us keep it simple and assume they remain constant. We will also assume our property grows in value at 4 per cent as per the previous case study.

What is the impact of borrowing for the two options?

Linda will make an extra $21,720 in repayments over the 10-year period. Her projected loan balance at the date of the sale is more than Sarah's.

While Linda will still make a greater after-tax capital gain than Sarah, due to the extra repayments and loan balance, her pre-tax profit will not be as great as it was in the first example.

In summary, although Sarah has been able to use a higher

tax rate when offsetting any annual losses, Linda has enjoyed a much lower tax rate on the capital gains.

I would stress this is a very simple example designed to show the difference in how the two options work. It ignores issues such as the cost of buying and selling the property, tax deductible contributions being used to repay the debt, annual net income and its tax effect.

The difference between the outcomes for the two examples are dependent very much on the assumptions.

And once their properties have been sold, then what?

Having sold their properties, where does that leave Linda and Sarah?

Sarah has her profits sitting in her bank account waiting to be invested. Any income she earns, including future capital gains will be taxable at marginal tax rates. In retirement she will be entitled to various benefits such as the Senior Australian Tax Offset. However, it is important to note these offsets are designed for people on lower incomes, not for people on higher incomes looking to replace their pre-retirement salary with an equivalent amount post retirement.

Linda, on the other hand, has her profits in her SMSF and we have already seen how favourably they will be taxed there.

Where would I rather have my investments at retirement – in an SMSF!

Key Points

- Comparing investing in property through an SMSF with investing as an individual is not always straightforward. A number of assumptions must be made and individual circumstances taken into account.

- The amount of tax you pay on your investment in each scenario will depend on many variables; your age and the phase of your SMSF, your total income and the desired outcome for the investment – i.e. for capital gain or to generate income.

CHAPTER 11

Property partners

WE'VE ALL heard the expression, "There's safety in numbers", and this can ring true with property investing. In some circumstances, it makes sense not to go at it alone but to seek an investing partner. Often, considering going down the partnership route is due to the size of the investment being too large for one individual. Or it could be that business partners are looking to acquire new premises together.

Partnerships can be made up of people and entities and, of course, one (or both) entity can be a self managed super fund. An SMSF can purchase property with one or more parties (either with cash or with borrowings) in either of the following ways. The fund can:

- enter into a partnership with the other party; or
- establish a trust into which all of the parties invest.

Although there are legal differences between a trust and a partnership, the outcome is essentially the same: the SMSF plus one or more parties acquire a property together. Also, depending on the property acquired, the fund could well have the opportunity of acquiring the other parties' interests at some future date.

However, before proceeding down this path, you will need to ask your accountant or financial adviser to check that the proposed arrangement complies with superannuation legislation. This will ensure that your SMSF does not find itself in breach of the law and facing a very expensive exit from what should have been a profitable investment.

Partnerships

A partnership in its simplest form consists of two parties agreeing to own (for the purposes of the discussion in this book) a property. They agree to share the costs, income and the profits from the investment upon its sale.

While most property in a partnership arrangement is split 50/50 between the two parties, this is not a legal requirement. In practice, it is what each of the parties can afford that will determine how much each party owns.

Let's take a look at an example of an SMSF buying property in partnership with someone else.

Example

Diana and Midhun have their own SMSF with $300,000 in cash available to invest. They would like to purchase a residential property with a sale price of $500,000. They're not keen on their fund borrowing to supplement the shortfall. Diana and Midhun have savings outside of their super of $300,000 in cash between them and they are also in a position to borrow against the family home.

They opt to buy the property in partnership with their SMSF. As both parties can pay 50 per cent of costs (the price plus expenses involved in purchasing the property) they opt for a 50/50 partnership.

In this scenario, both parties (the SMSF and Diana and Midhun) are entitled to a half share of the rental income and are liable for half of the expenses associated with the property.

As mentioned previously there is no requirement for a 50/50 split and if the SMSF had $400,000 in cash it could well have acquired a larger interest in the property.

It is important, especially when an SMSF is involved, to keep track of the income and expenses associated with a property investment. (Please see Chapter 14 on record-keeping.)

I would recommend a separate bank account be established for the partnership. Rental income would go into this account and expenses would come out of it and each year a payment of net income (incomings minus outgoings) should be paid to the two investment partners.

Alternatively, the property could be leased out via an estate agent and any rental income would be paid to the agent. Once the agent's fees and costs are deducted, the net rent could then be paid into either a joint investors' bank account or separate bank accounts. My preference, however, would be for a separate joint bank account to cover unforeseen consequences.

Although it is not necessary to document a partnership, I would, however, recommend that when an SMSF is involved, the interests of each party be recorded. This may be a minute at a meeting or it may be a simple, written partnership agreement between the owners confirming what share each party owns and what is to happen to rental income and expenses.

Keep in mind that any decision to purchase property in partnership with your fund will need to be documented in the minutes of your next SMSF trustee meeting. The minutes should note the decision to acquire the property, naming the parties as well as their entitlements.

Your SMSF auditor will also want to sight these minutes, along with the contract of sale and the title to the property.

Buying a partner out

As your superannuation fund grows, it could purchase your share of the property or, alternatively, you may wish to acquire your fund's portion of the property.

Irrespective of who buys who out, the process involves a cash payment and will incur stamp duty. It will be viewed as a 'disposal', and as such it may well incur capital gains tax (CGT) should a profit result from the transaction.

Alternatively, fund members could transfer their portion of the property, if allowable, as an *in specie* contribution to their SMSF. Under this scenario, as no cash has effectively changed hands, in some states stamp duty will be minimal. It is important the solicitor handling the property transfer advise you here.

Acquiring the other party's interest is not always straightforward.

Let's go back to our example to see what happened to Diana and Midhun.

Example (cont'd)

Diana and Midhun's SMSF is now large enough to purchase their share of the investment property. However, because the property is residential, superannuation legislation prevents the SMSF from purchasing Diana and Midhun's (the fund members') share, because they are 'associated' to the fund. (This provision also extends to family members and trusts or companies with whom members are associated. It was introduced as a result of SMSFs paying above market prices to acquire residential property from members.)

Although Diana and Midhun's SMSF cannot purchase their share of the property, the law doesn't prevent them buying their fund's interest in the property, provided it is purchased at market price. Any profit will, however, be subject to CGT.

Had Diana and Midhun and their SMSF partnered to purchase commercial property that met the 'business real property test' the fund could have acquired the couple's interest further down the track. According to the test, property must be used for business purposes prior or at the time of purchase and can be a shop, factory, offices or farmland. Even a house used for business purposes would qualify (please see Chapter 5).

As a humorous aside, several years ago an SMSF trustee asked if her fund could purchase a house she owned. The property was being used for business purposes and the rental was way in excess of what would normally be generated by residential property. On investigation, I discovered a brothel was operating out of the house!

Using borrowings to fund a partnership

Should you need to borrow to buy your share of a property, you could use the family home as security for a loan. However, you cannot use the actual property being purchased as security. In essence, this is an asset of the SMSF and cannot be used as security for personal borrowings. If this occurs, the fund could lose its concessional (pre-tax) rate of 15 per cent and have this replaced by a more draconian 46.5 per cent.

From time to time I have come across situations where those partnering SMSFs have wanted to borrow and the lender has suggested the property being purchased be used as security for the debt. Often the lender will want security over the whole property or over the non SMSF partner's interest in the property.

Be wary of blindly following a request of this nature.

Selling a share in the property

The problem with going into partnership is that partners do not always agree. What happens when your partner either needs, or wants, to sell his or her share in the property you are investing in together to a third-party? You may not be happy about this.

In theory, this is possible but in practice it can be problematic, particularly if the new purchaser has to borrow to finance his or her share of the property.

It is also problematic because the purchaser will only buy a part interest in the property, eliminating many potential buyers. In these circumstances the most likely purchaser will probably be someone the existing partner knows.

Let's go back to our example to illustrate this.

Example (cont'd)

Returning to Diana and Midhun, they are looking to sell their share of the property they purchased with their fund because they want to free up money to start a business.

The jointly-owned asset is a residential property and their fund is unable to purchase their interest. If a replacement partner cannot be found the property will have to be sold.

A solution would be to have a family member such as Diana's sister, Flora, purchase Diana and Midhun's share. Flora owns her own home and can borrow using her home as security. However, keep in mind that because she is Diana's relative (and therefore an 'associate'), the fund will not be able to buy her share of the property at some future date.

What if a commercial property such as a shop had been purchased instead of a house?

In theory, this could make it easier for the fund to buy Flora's share in the property further down the track. However, at the time Flora wants to sell, the SMSF might not have the cash available to acquire her interest. It might also discard this proposition due to problems with diversification if it is already invested in other properties. Furthermore, as the property is already part owned by the SMSF, it could not borrow using the property as security.

Partnering using a trust

A trust is a separate legal entity that can be established to own the property all parties wish to acquire. Unlike partnerships, where partners typically hold equal shares, participants in trusts may invest differing amounts and the number of units issued to each participant can vary.

The trustee would typically be a company in which all of the investors hold a share and are directors. Having a trustee company operate the trust can be easier than having the partners responsible for all decision-making.

Trusts are often selected to invest jointly in property because they are easier to operate than partnerships. At the end of each financial year, investors receive their share of income (proportionate to the number of units they hold in the trust), once expenses have been deducted, just as they would if there had been a partnership.

As trusts operate as a separate entity, this makes altering ownership arrangements much easier. The title of the property is in the trustee's name, rather than in the names of all the participants. So when exiting, investors can sell to another party without requiring any changes to be made to the title. Sale of units doesn't impact on the property ownership as you are selling units in the trust rather than shares in the property.

Setting up a unit trust

How does the process of setting up a unit trust work? Let's use an example of Adrian and four friends (who decide to buy a property together) to explain the process.

Example

The property the group wants to buy is valued at $600,000, including the costs associated with the purchase, such as stamp duty. They opt for a unit trust structure, with each of the friends acquiring 120,000 units at $1 each – effectively contributing $120,000 towards the purchase of the property.

Adrian decides to buy his units via his SMSF which has $120,000 in available cash. His friends decide to use their personal savings.

Assuming there are no borrowings in the unit trust, there will be no restrictions on Adrian's SMSF investing in the trust. Distributions from the trust – being the net rental income – would be subject to the 15 per cent tax rate enjoyed by superannuation funds.

Instead of buying units equal to the value of the property being purchased, the five friends could invest money in the trust and have the trust borrow in order to purchase the property.

The borrowings required to purchase the property would be in the name of the trustee.

Note: If there are going to be borrowings, any SMSF participating in the trust should determine whether or not the investment will place the fund in breach of superannuation legislation. I would suggest you speak to your accountant or superannuation adviser if you are uncertain.

The potential for breaches when using trusts

It is important to be mindful of breaches as these could occur if the SMSF investing in the trust owns more than 50 per cent of the trust's units or has more than 50 per cent of the voting rights of the trust. Should the combined interests of the SMSF and any associated parties in a trust exceed the 50 per cent thresholds, the SMSF could also be in breach as a result of investing in the trust. An associated party could be another of the SMSF's members and/or a relative of the member. If the 50 per cent threshold is exceeded, the SMSF will face restrictions on the level of its investment should the trust decide to use borrowings to acquire the property. If you are uncertain I strongly recommend you obtain advice.

You don't want to discover you are in breach and that:

- the tax rate on your fund's income has gone from 15 per cent to 46.5 per cent; and
- your fund and the property or trust you have invested in has to be separated, your fund's interest sold, and significant costs and losses are incurred along the way.

It was proposed, from July 2013, that changes to superannuation legislation would see the introduction of a new administrative penalty regime. This would allow the ATO to impose financial penalties on the trustee of an SMSF for breaches of legislation. (This legislation was not passed prior to the 2013 Federal Election and it was still to be re-introduced to Parliament at the time of writing.)

Other SMSF partnership possibilities

So far my comments have been reserved to SMSFs partnering with fund members or trusts to acquire property. There are other alternatives, such as SMSFs partnering with:

- a family trust;
- a company owned by fund members;
- relatives or friends of fund members;
- trusts or companies of associates (relatives, friends or business associates);
- another SMSF.

Let's look at these scenarios below.

Family trusts

Self managed superannuation fund members may have a family trust which they use to operate a business or as an investment vehicle. They may decide to form a partnership between the SMSF and the family trust for purposes of investing in property. One reason for doing this might be the flexibility family trusts offer for income distribution. Because a family trust is a discretionary trust (i.e. the trustee determines how the capital and income will be distributed among beneficiaries), income can be distributed to different people each year. Restrictions will apply if the family trust wants to sell to the SMSF because both partners are 'associated'.

Company owned by the fund members

Your SMSF may consider forming an investment partnership with a company. This may seem an attractive proposal if your company wants to buy commercial property and perhaps rent these as business premises. One disadvantage to this strategy is that the company is not eligible for a capital gains tax discount when the property is sold. However, this may be outweighed by other advantages of this partnership.

Friends or relatives

Where friends or relatives are invited to partner with your fund by investing directly in the property or investing via a company or trust, you need to ensure they have the same objectives and goals as your SMSF. For example, if your plans are to buy the property, receive rent for the next ten years and then sell, you don't want a partner who will want the money within the next four to five years. I would also suggest that when you partner with friends or relatives you still need to adopt a commercial approach. Keep agreements in writing and minute any changes along the way.

Friend or relative's SMSF

Investing with a friend or a relative's SMSF means the interests of both funds will have to be closely aligned. Both will need to agree they are investing for the longer term – that is, to provide a nest-egg for SMSF members in their retirement.

One potential problem with this type of partnership is where there is a significant age difference between members of each fund. One couple may have reached their late fifties and the other couple may only be in their forties. What could happen in this scenario is that if the property were to be sold, the older couple could well be receiving an income stream from their fund which means they would not have to pay capital gains tax on the profit of the sale. The younger couple however would be liable for CGT on their share of any profits.

It is important to discuss your SMSF partnering to invest in property with your adviser.

Key Points

- For larger property investments a good strategy could be to invest with a partner.
- Partners can be individuals, trusts, companies or other SMSFs.
- There are pros and cons for each prospective partnership.
- There is also legislation that affects some of these partnerships which you need to be sure you don't breach.

CHAPTER 12

Retirement and property

WHEN SELF managed super fund members reach retirement there are many options open to them. It is definitely a good idea to discuss your transition to retirement with your adviser or financial planner – well before you reach your retirement date.

In this chapter we look at the various retirement options available to SMSF members and how these options will impact those who have purchased property via their funds.

Note: some of my commentary is also applicable to fund members who have reached preservation age (currently 55 but rising to 60 by 2024) at which time they can commence an income stream from their fund without having to retire.

What happens at retirement?

Upon retirement, superannuants essentially have three ways that they can access their super savings:

- they can take out a lump sum;
- start a pension or income stream;
- take out a combination of the two.

For many, the first option is the most realistic one because the only contributions to their super will have come from their employers and will have been restricted to the compulsory contributions (9.25 per cent of salary from July 2013). As a result many will be retiring with relatively small fund balances. For those who have taken advantage of the tax benefits available to super funds and have made additional contributions where possible and invested in quality investments, the other two options may also be appropriate.

To get an understanding of what is involved with each option, let's examine all three through the prism of Steven who, at the age of 60, decides to retire. His SMSF has a balance of $1.2 million.

Example: Option 1 – The lump sum

With this option Steven takes his super balance out in full as a lump sum. Thanks to legislative changes in July 2007, now that he is 60 he will no longer pay tax on any lump sum benefits.

However, any investments which Steven may have sold and converted into cash, or any investments that have been transferred to him as part of his benefits, will be subject to capital gains tax (CGT). This amount will have to be deducted before the lump sum can be paid to him.

When Steven invests this lump sum outside of super and receives an income from the investment, the income will be taxed at his personal marginal tax rates. Also, any realised capital gains from this investment activity will be taxed according to CGT rules for individuals.

Do keep in mind that if an individual sells or redeems an investment and has owned the investment for less than twelve months, the full capital gain is taxable at marginal tax rates. However, when the investment has been held for more than twelve months, 50 per cent of the capital gain will be tax exempt.

Example: Option 2 – Pension or income stream

If Steven takes a pension or income stream from his SMSF upon retirement, as he is the only member and is using his entire account balance to provide himself with an income, neither the fund nor Steven will be liable for further tax.

While prior to commencing an income stream the fund was taxed at 15 per cent, once the fund starts paying Steven a retirement income stream, the tax rate drops to zero. As a result 100 per cent of Steven's income, including any realised capital gains, will not be subject to tax.

This type of pension paid from an SMSF in Option 2 is known as an 'account-based pension', with either part – or the entire balance on retiring – being used to provide an income. This can continue to be paid until:

- all the money in the account has been used up; or
- the member dies; or
- the 'reversionary' pensioner dies.

A reversionary pensioner is the person you nominate to receive your pension account's remaining balance when you die. This could be your spouse or partner but cannot be a child unless they are either:

- less than 18 years of age,
- between age 18 and 25 and financially dependent on you immediately prior to your death; or
- permanently disabled.

Assuming there is money remaining in the account, once both the member and reversionary pensioner have died, this can be paid directly to dependants of the reversionary pensioner or to pensioner's estate.

Example: Option 3 – Combination of both

The third option for Steven would be to take a combination of lump sum and income stream. He could take $200,000 as a lump sum benefit which could be used to pay off the mortgage on his home and take an overseas holiday, and the remaining $1 million could be used to provide an income stream during retirement.

Provided the lump sum is paid without having to sell or redeem investments (which would be subject to CGT), neither the fund nor Steven will have to pay tax on the lump sum or pension payments.

Coming up to retirement, Steven may have identified the need to take some of his benefits as a lump sum but he may not want to redeem investments at that time and as a result have a capital gains tax liability. To avoid being in this position Steven could decide to direct contributions and investment earnings in the twelve months to two years prior to retirement, for example, to short-term fixed interest investments. He will then be able to use these investments to pay the lump sum benefit.

What happens to property on retiring?

Now let's look specifically at what happens to your property investments when you retire.

There are several options available.

Hold the property

There is no requirement for a property to be sold when you retire. Your SMSF can continue to hold on to the property and the fund can still receive rental income. This income can be used to assist in funding your lifestyle in retirement.

Transfer the property

The fund could transfer the property to you as an *in specie* lump sum benefit and this could be used as part of your retirement benefit. If you were to go down this path, the property would need to be transferred as a lump sum benefit and will be deemed a 'disposal' for CGT purposes. As a result, the fund will incur CGT on two-thirds of any profit made. In some states and territories, stamp duty may also be payable on the transfer. We would suggest advice be first obtained before making any property transfer.

Sell and take out a lump sum

A third alternative would be to sell the property upon retirement and this amount could be added to your lump sum benefit. Alternatively you could retain the proceeds within the fund, purchase other investments and use the income generated to provide you with a pension.

Sell and start an income stream

Another option would be to sell the property at some later date when you have started receiving a pension or income stream.

The million dollar question is which is the best option to choose?

The answer: it will depend on your individual circumstances.

Looking at the options above, let's see how these work in practice. I will assume that in all these scenarios the property was purchased for $400,000 over twelve months ago and is now valued at $500,000.

Leaving your property in your SMSF

There is no requirement to make any changes to your superannuation fund upon retirement. You can choose to leave your property in your SMSF and you don't have to take money from your fund when you retire.

After retiring you can continue investing at the same low tax rate of 15 per cent even if you don't commence a pension or income stream. Your property will continue to earn rental income with expenses such as rates being offset against this prior to calculating the tax due.

If you decide to keep the property and commence a pension or income stream from your SMSF, you would need to give careful consideration to your fund being able to keep up its commitment to the pension or income stream while still holding the property. Should there be insufficient cash to do so, you may have to sell the property at what could be an inconvenient time.

Transferring the property as an *in specie* lump sum benefit

Having retired you may decide to transfer the ownership of the property to yourself. This may be because you've decided to close the super fund or because you've decided the property is to become your principal place of residence. Remember, your SMSF cannot own your residential home. Transferring the property is regarded as a 'disposal' for capital gains tax purposes.

You will have to pay tax on the $100,000 realised profit – the difference between the cost price of $400,000 and the current value of $500,000. All up, you will be liable for a CGT bill of $10,000.

How do we arrive at this figure?

Keep in mind that when property is owned by a super fund for more than twelve months, one-third of the profit will not be taxed. Because your SMSF is not paying a pension or income stream, tax on capital gains is calculated at 15 per cent. If it had been paying you an income stream there would be no tax payable (see following example).

The tax calculation is: two-thirds of $100,000 x 15 per cent, giving $10,000 as the amount to be paid from the fund.

Selling the property on retirement and taking a lump sum benefit

Instead of transferring ownership to yourself, you may decide to sell the property upon retirement. This could be with the intention of adding the sale proceeds to your lump sum benefit.

You will be liable for CGT which would be the same as when property is transferred to a member (i.e. $10,000 – see previous example).

Selling your property once you begin receiving a pension or income stream

On retiring you may decide to keep your SMSF operational and take an income from it. Once a pension or income stream is being paid, the fund will no longer be liable for tax and if you are 60 or more, your pension will not be taxed.

However, if you are aged between 55 and 59, part, or all, of your pension would be subject to tax. Later in this chapter we will see how this is calculated.

While you are receiving an income from your fund, the property can be retained as an asset within the fund or sold. In fact, it can be sold as soon as one day after the pension or income stream commences.

Going back to Steven, because his fund is now paying a pension and he is the only member of the SMSF and he has retired, the fund's income is exempt from tax. What this means is when his fund eventually sells the property and makes a profit on the sale, there will be no capital gains tax on the profit. Where Steven is concerned, this will save his fund $10,000 in tax.

It is important to point out that if you have taken a combination of a lump sum and an income stream, you may have to pay tax when you sell the property. This could take the form of CGT within the fund and for someone aged between 55 and 59 there may be some personal tax on the benefit received from the sale of the property too.

I would recommend you obtain advice from your accountant prior to selling the property if you plan to go down this route.

As can be seen from the above examples, from a tax perspective it is better to be retired and receiving an income or pension before going ahead and selling any investment properties owned through your SMSF.

Tax on retirement benefits

While the section above addresses the CGT implications of selling property, do keep in mind – depending on your age – you may also have to pay tax on the benefits you withdraw from your fund on retiring.

According to current superannuation rules, if you are 60 or more you will not have to pay tax, irrespective of whether you receive a lump sum or a pension from your fund.

However, if you are between 55 and 59, you will have to pay tax, whichever option you take. However, having said that, part of your benefit may be tax exempt.

Why so?

Keep in mind that prior to starting an income stream, your super fund is divided into two components – taxable and tax exempt.

- The **taxable component** is made up of concessional (pre-tax) contributions such as the compulsory amounts employers have to pay into employees' superannuation funds plus any amounts contributed as a result of salary sacrificing arrangements. For self-employed people and those operating businesses through a company or trust, this is the tax deductible contribution paid as part of tax and retirement planning. All income earned by the fund prior to a benefit being paid is included in the taxable component of your account balance.
- The **tax-exempt component** comprises non-concessional (after-tax) contributions for which NO tax deduction has been claimed. These can only be made by fund members (not employers).

In certain circumstances, the tax-exempt amount will be increased. This will occur if you have made contributions as a result of the small business CGT rollover concessions or you have what is called an 'eligible service date' of earlier than 30 June 1983. The former can only be applicable if you have previously operated your own business while the latter will only apply if you were in the workforce prior to 30 June 1983.

I would suggest that if you are operating your own business you speak to your accountant prior to selling the business and retiring. This way you'll get the best advice about the small business CGT rollover concessions and how they would apply to you.

If you meet the eligible service date requirements, your tax-exempt component would have been automatically adjusted by the fund's administrator at June 2007.

Returning to Steven, let's take a look at how his retirement benefits will be taxed should he take a lump sum or pension/income stream. Steven's $1.2 million superannuation balance is broken up as follows:

- $200,000 worth of non-concessional (after-tax) contributions. This portion is tax exempt.
- $1 million in concessional (pre-tax) contributions which are taxable.

Example: Scenario 1: Lump sum

Let's assume Steven takes a lump sum benefit using his entire account balance. If Steven was 60 when he retired, he would pay no tax on the benefit from the fund. However, if he retired when he was between 55 and 59, the tax treatment of the taxable component (the $1 million) would be:

- He would not have to pay tax on the first $180,000 if he retired in the 2013-14 financial year. Everyone is entitled to receive this amount of taxable benefits as a lump sum benefit, once they have reached preservation age and meet the conditions of release[#]. This figure is indexed annually based on the movement in *Average Weekly Ordinary Times Earnings.*

- The remaining $820,000 would be taxed at 15 per cent. Steven would also have to pay a Medicare levy.

- All up, he would be liable for a tax bill of $135,300

[#] Conditions of release are that superannuation fund members aged between 55-59 are required to be retired from the work-force; while those aged 60-64 must have ceased a period of employment. No conditions apply once fund members reach 65.

There would be no further tax paid on the balance of the fund, i.e. the $200,000 non-concessional contributions.

Example: Scenario 2: Pension/income stream

If Steven retires at 60 or older, he will not pay tax on money he receives as a pension or income stream from his super fund. However, if he retires aged between 55 and 59 and elects to take a pension or income stream there would be some tax payable.

Let's assume Steven takes $48,000 in his first year of retirement (4 per cent of his account balance). This is the minimum percentage for someone aged between 55 and 64.

As $200,000 (or one-sixth of his account balance) is the tax-exempt component (made up of non-concessional contributions) when he commences a pension, then one-sixth of the pension paid each year will always be tax exempt.

One-sixth of the first year's pension equates to $8,000, leaving $40,000 subject to income tax.

Let's take a look at how much tax he will have to pay each year.

Under these circumstances, income tax is payable at marginal tax rates less the 15 per cent tax rebate*. Assuming Steven has no other income in the year, his tax will be:

First $18,200:	Nil
$18,201 – $37,000:	$3,572 (19% tax rate)
$37,001 – $40,000:	$ 975 (32.5% tax rate)
Medicare levy:	$ 600 (1.5% of $40,000)
Less rebate*:	$4,547
Amount payable:	$ 600

* The rebate is 15 per cent of the taxable component of the pension or the amount of tax payable calculated at marginal tax rates but excluding the Medicare levy whichever is the lesser. In this example, 15 per cent of the taxable component is $6,000 which is higher than the tax payable.

With his fund providing him with an income, Steven has created a tax effective income stream for himself. He does not pay tax on his income of $48,000, and the Medicare levy is payable on only part of his income.

This allows Steven to retain ownership of the investment property in his SMSF even when he has retired. Subject to him being able to pay the required pension or income stream each year, he can keep the property in the fund well into retirement until he decides to sell.

Key Points

- Upon retirement, and approaching retirement there are strategies that you can use to reduce the amount of tax you pay (under some circumstances to nil).

- Taking out an income stream often may be the most tax effective way to access superannuation savings.

- When you sell any property accumulated by your SMSF could make a considerable difference to the tax you will pay.

Succession planning

NO-ONE LIKES to think about death but the reality is that we need to ensure that our hard-earned assets are passed on after we are no longer here. In the previous chapter we looked at what happens to the properties we've purchased with our funds when we retire. In this chapter we will look at what happens when we die and there are still assets, including property, in our SMSFs.

This is an extremely complex area, so we will focus on how to prepare generally for the eventuality, looking at the rules relating to who can receive the deceased's benefits and how these benefits will be paid out.

One thing to be aware of is that property purchased in your own name can be included in your will but investments in your SMSF cannot, and as a result, require separate treatment. So just as it is important to keep your wills up to date where your personal assets are concerned, it is also necessary that you give thought to what will happen to your SMSF assets when you die.

Death benefit nomination options

When it comes to who will determine how your SMSF benefits will be allocated, you have three options. You can:

1. Leave the decision to the other fund trustees
2. Recommend to the trustees who you would like the benefits to go to
3. Instruct trustees on who the benefits must be paid to.

Option 1 – Leave the decision to other fund trustees

If you haven't made a 'death benefit nomination', the trustees will make the decision on your passing and could pay your death benefits to anyone who qualifies as a beneficiary under superannuation legislation. This would include 'tax dependants' – a spouse (current or former), a bona fide de facto, a child under age 18, people in an interdependency relationship, as well as adult children, parents and your legal personal representative (the executor of your estate).

Option 2 – Recommend how benefits be paid

By completing a 'non-binding death benefit nomination' you are able to indicate how you would like your death benefits to be distributed. Although this nomination isn't binding it is considered when benefits are apportioned.

As you are only recommending your preferred beneficiary, your trustee may follow your suggestion or alternatively decide to give the money to another beneficiary. This could be as a result of changed circumstances, particularly where a nomination was made some time ago and relationships or dependencies have changed. The trustee may also take into consideration the tax implications of the distribution.

Providing your trustees have complied with superannuation legislation in reaching their decision, 'preferred beneficiaries' nominated in the 'non-binding death nomination' but overlooked by trustees, will not be able to mount a successful claim against the decision.

Several years ago there was a court case in Australia (Katz v Grossmann) concerning the super entitlements of the father of two adult children. One of the children was a trustee with her father. In his non-binding death nomination, the father advised that he wanted his death benefit split equally between his children. His trustee daughter decided otherwise. After appointing her husband as the second trustee, she decided to take all the benefits herself. During the ensuing court case, the court agreed with the decision because it had been made in accordance with superannuation legislation.

Option 3 – Instruct how benefits be paid

The third option is called a 'binding death benefit nomination.' This is a formal document which enables you to determine precisely who will receive your death benefit (provided they are dependants and/or your legal personal representative).

From my experience over many years this type of nomination ensures benefits are paid in accordance with your wishes and avoids conflict among beneficiaries.

A couple of years ago I was invited to advise on a death benefit regarding a single member fund. The husband had died some years earlier and his widow had recently passed away. Control of the superannuation fund had fallen into the hands of one of the widow's sons. With no binding nomination in place and a fund with assets in excess of $2 million, there must have been enormous temptation for the son to hold onto the benefits himself. Fortunately, commonsense prevailed and he decided to share the funds equally with his brother and sister. You can only begin to imagine the bitterness that would have ensued had he not done the right thing.

Lapsing and non-lapsing nominations

Unlike retail or industry superannuation funds – where nominations lapse after three years – SMSF nominations can be either 'lapsing' or 'non-lapsing'. If they are lapsing they must be updated after three years. If they are non-lapsing they will remain intact indefinitely unless changed by the relevant fund member.

However, don't automatically assume your SMSF can make non-lapsing nominations. This must be provided for in the SMSF's trust deed. If non-lapsing nominations are not provided for, I would suggest you arrange with your solicitor or superannuation adviser for your fund's trust deed to be amended.

Do keep in mind that binding nominations can be altered at any time and it is important that they are kept up to date should circumstances change and the 'wrong' person ends up with your superannuation benefits.

Failure to make changes happens more frequently than you would care to imagine.

One case we came across involved an SMSF member who had made his first wife his beneficiary when he started his fund. He had forgotten to update his binding death nomination when he divorced her and took up with a new partner with whom he subsequently had a child. Had he died suddenly, his former wife would have been entitled to all his superannuation benefits. Luckily this oversight was picked up and his new dependants are his beneficiaries.

To avoid potential problems, I suggest you speak to either or both your superannuation adviser and your solicitor.

Rules regarding beneficiaries

The payment of superannuation benefits is further complicated by who the beneficiaries are. There are differing rules for taxing benefits when the beneficiary is:

- a spouse or a tax dependant;
- neither a spouse nor a tax dependant.

A tax dependant includes a spouse (current or former), a bona fide de facto, a child under age 18, and people in an 'interdependency' relationship.

An interdependency relationship is defined as a close personal relationship between two people who live together, where one or both provides financial and domestic support and personal care for the other. Two examples are a same sex couple and an adult child living with his or her widowed parent.

Individuals maintaining a close personal relationship but not living together due to physical, intellectual or psychiatric disability are also considered to have an 'interdependency relationship'.

A son or daughter aged between 18 and 25 could be considered a tax dependant. However, this will depend on individual circumstances, for example, if they are in full-time employment they are no longer deemed tax dependants.

Note: Benefits can also be paid to the member's legal personal representative and form part of the deceased's estate. If this occurs, subsequent payment of the benefits would be governed by the deceased's will.

According to superannuation legislation, upon death, benefits can either be paid to beneficiaries:

- in the form of a lump sum benefit; or, in certain instances;
- as a pension or income stream.

However, a pension can only be paid to a spouse/de facto or a tax dependant.

Should there be property in the SMSF, beneficiaries meeting the definition of spouse or tax dependant, can retain the property in the fund and draw an income or pension from the SMSF. Alternatively, they can elect to take the benefit as a lump sum.

However, where the beneficiary is not a tax dependant, benefits must be paid as a lump sum.

It is important to keep in mind that each SMSF is governed by a trust deed which determines how a benefit can be paid. Check with your superannuation adviser who will be best able to advise you.

Tax implications for beneficiaries

If the SMSF either has a reversionary pensioner or a beneficiary who is eligible to receive benefits by way of a pension, and elects to do so, then an income stream would continue to be paid. The SMSF would remain exempt from tax whilst this occurs.

However, if a lump sum benefit has to be paid the pension ceases. In early 2013, the government announced it would allow the CGT exemptions of a pension paying fund to continue when a member in receipt of a pension had died and the benefits were to be paid either to the deceased's estate or his/her beneficiaries as a lump sum. The only requirement was that payment of the benefits had to be made within a reasonable period of time.

If we consider an SMSF which held property at the date of death of the last member, previously CGT would have been payable by the SMSF if either the property was sold or transferred to the beneficiaries. CGT will no longer apply in these circumstances.

However, eligible termination payment (ETP) tax may still be payable on lump sum benefits that go to a non-tax dependant. This tax should be deducted by the SMSF trustee prior to paying the beneficiary. The 16.5 per cent tax rate, which includes the Medicare levy, only applies to the 'taxable' component of the benefit. The taxable and non-taxable components are calculated as follows:

- If the deceased had not been receiving an income or pension from the SMSF at the time of death the tax-exempt component would be the sum of any non-concessional (after-tax) contributions made to the fund. This amount is deducted from the total of the member's account with the balance being the taxable component.

- If a pension or income stream was being paid at the time of death, a calculation is required to have been made at the time the pension commenced, determining what percentage of the member's balance is taxable and what isn't. The tax-exempt percentage would be a total of the non-concessional (after-tax) contributions expressed as a percentage of the member's account balance at the time the pension commenced.

If the beneficiary is entitled to receive the deceased's benefits as a pension or income stream, taxes can be ignored, provided, of course, he or she actually does commence a pension from the fund. A benefit can only be paid in this way if the beneficiary is a spouse or tax dependant.

The tax treatment of benefits paid as a pension will vary according to the age of the recipient:

- When a benefit goes to a spouse or tax dependant who is 60 or more, the benefit will be tax exempt.

- When the benefit goes to a spouse or tax dependant aged under 60, and the initial pensioner was aged 60 or more at the time of death, the benefit will be tax exempt.

- When the benefit goes to a spouse or tax dependant under 60 and the initial pensioner was aged under 60 at the date of death, tax is payable on the taxable percentage which would have been calculated at the time the member started a pension (refer above):

  - If the person is aged between 55 and 59 years, the tax is calculated at the recipient's marginal tax rates with a 15 per cent tax rebate applying to the taxable pension received.

  - If the person is less than 55 but not under 25, tax is calculated on the person's marginal tax rate.

  - For children under 25, income tax will be payable at marginal tax rates. Once the child turns 25, the remaining account balance has to be taken as a tax-free lump sum.

If the deceased was not receiving a pension at the time of death and the beneficiary elected – if eligible – to take the benefit as a pension, the trustee would need to determine what percentage of the pension would be taxable and non-taxable.

To do this, trustees need to calculate how much of the member's account comprised non-concessional (after-tax) contributions. These would be tax free whereas the balance of the account would be taxable.

By way of example should the member have made non-concessional contributions of $100,000 and the account balance at the start of the pension was $500,000, then 80 per cent of the pension payable would be subject to income tax if the recipient was under 60.

Death and your SMSF property

Now that you have determined who your beneficiaries will be and what the tax implications will be for them, let's turn our attention to what will happen to properties in your SMSF should you die.

There are three courses of action that the trustee can take:

- sell the property;
- transfer the property to a beneficiary;
- retain the property within the fund.

The last option is only available if a pension is to be paid to the beneficiary.

Selling the property

At the time of death, if the member was not in receipt of a pension or income stream from their SMSF, CGT will be payable on the sale of the property if any capital gain has been made.

If the property was owned for less than twelve months at

the time of sale, all profits will be taxed. However, if the property was owned for more than twelve months, tax will only apply to two-thirds of the profit.

If the member was receiving a pension, then as we have seen above, CGT would not be applicable.

What happens if there are two members at the date of death and a property is to be sold in order to pay a lump sum benefit?

For funds where both members are in receipt of a pension/income stream, no CGT would be payable. But if one was a pensioner and the other in accumulation mode, and the member in accumulation mode died, then:

- If the assets were not segregated between pensioner and non pensioner members, an actuary would determine the percentage subject to tax.
- If the assets were segregated and the property was being sold to pay the lump sum benefit, then 15 per cent tax would be levied on two-thirds of the realised gain.

I would suggest trustees speak to their accountants about 'segregating' assets. There may be benefits to be obtained and there will be extra costs. Segregating assets involves allocating assets between pension accounts and accumulation accounts. Using this approach, trustees could allocate specific assets to each type of account. This would affect the rate of tax applied.

Transferring the property to a beneficiary

Until recently, transferring the property to a beneficiary was considered a 'disposal' for capital gains tax purposes, with any profit being taxed 15 per cent.

Thanks to the government's announcement earlier in 2013, provided the deceased was in receipt of a superannuation pension at the date of death, CGT will not apply to the transfer.

However, as we noted, eligible termination payment (ETP) tax may be payable on the taxable component of the total benefit paid if the beneficiary was not a tax dependant of the deceased.

Retaining the property within the fund

This option assumes the beneficiary is eligible for, and elects to receive, a pension from the fund. In this instance the property can remain within the fund's ownership and continue generating income by way of the rent.

Because the fund will be paying an income stream, the fund's income will be tax exempt assuming there is only one member in the fund. If, at the time of death, there are two members (the now deceased member and his/her spouse), part of the fund's income will be tax exempt should the surviving spouse's own account be in accumulation mode. The tax-exempt amount will be dependent on the relative size of the two accounts.

Let's use an example to better explain this.

Example:

Stephen and Mary are members of an SMSF. Mary is a tax dependant. Should Stephen die, she could elect to:

- Take both Stephen's and her benefits as a pension. However, to be eligible to do this, she must have reached preservation age (currently 55). If she has, the fund's income will not be taxed because pensions are being paid from the two members' accounts.

- If Mary hasn't reached preservation age, or decides not to start a pension from her account, only part of the fund's income will be tax exempt. This is because the fund has a pension paying account and an accumulation account. If the assets have not been segregated between the two accounts, the portion that will be tax-exempt income will have to be determined by an actuary. Your accountant or superannuation adviser will arrange for the necessary actuarial certificate to be obtained.

Key Points

- Property purchased in your SMSF cannot be included in your will.
- Your instructions on how to distribute benefits from your super fund should ideally be given in a binding death benefit nomination.
- Property can be retained in the fund after you die if your beneficiaries are a spouse and/or tax dependants and they are drawing an income from the fund.

CHAPTER 14

Compliance and record-keeping

SELF MANAGED super fund trustees have a range of responsibilities they must take care of in the day-to-day running of their funds, including the need for detailed record-keeping and making sure they comply with current legislation. This may not be the exciting part of managing your own super fund but it is nevertheless very important. With superannuation, as with most other things, ignorance is no defence.

In this chapter we start by taking a look at what SMSFs generally need to be doing in order to remain compliant. Then we discuss matters particularly relevant to trustees who hold property in their fund. Some of the compliance issues detailed below were covered in Chapter 2 on Setting up your SMSF, but it does no harm to remind you of them again here.

Complying with your fund's trust deed

As a trustee you are responsible for complying with the provisions of the trust deed governing your superannuation fund. The deed must provide details about fund trustees, how they have been appointed and their powers. It must also set out when and how contributions and benefits will be paid. You may find that you need to amend your trust deed from time to time. From discussions in early chapters you know that if your fund decides to borrow funds the trust deed needs to allow for this. As the members grow older, the deed may have to be amended to make death benefit nominations. It is a good idea to have your SMSF's trust deed reviewed at least once every five years.

GST registration and compliance

An SMSF investing in property must register for GST if its annual income from commercial property is greater than $75,000. If the income that is counted for GST purchases is less than $75,000, registration then becomes optional.

However, if it is optional for you to be registered for GST, I would suggest you discuss registration with your accountant. Sometimes registration, particularly when using an annual GST return, may be beneficial to your fund.

If your fund is registered for GST then you have to complete a business activity statement (BAS) every quarter. This will record the GST you have spent on expenses related to the maintenance and management of the property (and or other investments) and the GST the fund has collected. The difference between these two amounts will either result in a refund or the fund having to remit GST to the tax office.

GST is not payable on income received on the rent earned on residential properties.

Banking and money management

Has a separate bank account been set up for the fund? This

is very important to avoid contravening the *SIS Act*. A separate bank account prevents money which belongs to the fund from becoming mixed in with members' personal or business assets. Is this the best bank for your SMSF? There are several high interest cash management accounts on the market. It is a good idea to review bank accounts on a regular basis to ensure that your fund is paying the lowest fees and getting the highest interest on its cash deposits.

The assets of the fund must be kept separate from assets of members, trustees and related employers. Remember, your SMSF is a separate legal entity and should be kept well away from your personal affairs, your family trust and any businesses you are involved in.

To better enable this, your SMSF's assets (being its bank account and investments), should be held in the name of the fund trustee/s and the name of the fund should be recorded on documents relating to it. However, in some states the name of the SMSF cannot be recorded on the title for a property. In these circumstances, my suggestion would be for the trustee/s to pass a minute acknowledging the property has been acquired and is being held for your fund.

Your accountant, solicitor or superannuation adviser can assist you if required.

Accepting contributions

Are you aware of the rules regarding accepting contributions and which parties different types of contributions can come from? Concessional (pre-tax) contributions can be made by either an employer or by someone who is self-employed. In some instances, employees can make concessional contributions on top of those made by employers.

It is always wise to check with your accountant, prior to making any personal concessional contributions, to make sure that you are eligible to do so.

Non-concessional (after-tax) contributions can only be made by fund members (not employers).

Investment strategy

Your fund must have an investment strategy recorded when it is set up. Part of the responsibilities of trustees is to review the fund's investment strategy to ensure that investments have been made in accordance with this strategy. If not, the fund could incur penalties.

The strategy does not have to be lengthy or complicated. Many SMSFs operate with a one-pager. If you need assistance with drafting the strategy, speak to your accountant or financial planner. A fund is allowed to re-draft the strategy at any time, as long as changes are minuted.

Record-keeping

Trustees must keep records of transactions and the financial position of the fund. These include:

- Annual operating statements which must be kept for five years.
- Annual statements of the fund's legal position which must be held onto for five years.
- Copies of annual tax returns lodged for five years.
- Minutes of all meetings, records of trustee changes, records of director changes and written consent by members for trustee appointment. These must be kept for ten years.

Penalties apply if you fail to keep these records for the required time period. It is the responsibility of trustees to ensure adequate records are kept. These will be required when preparing and auditing superannuation accounts and to ensure a correct tax return is lodged.

Annual returns

Have you lodged your income tax and regulatory returns? Annual requirements also include appointing an auditor to examine the year's records and pay the supervisory levy.

Accounts must be prepared each year for the twelve months to 30 June. For an SMSF starting at any date after 1 July, the first return is from the start date to the next 30 June.

Do keep in mind that an SMSF must be audited prior to the annual return being lodged with the ATO. Normally your accountant or superannuation administrator will draft the accounts and annual return on your behalf. Regarding dates, your annual return must be lodged with the ATO by:

- 28th February, for the first year of operation;
- 15th May, for subsequent years.

Tax matters

Have you kept records of all the deductions, asset sales and purchases as well members' tax file numbers?

+ + +

The checklist above is not exhaustive. It does not cover everything you are required to know when managing your SMSF. For more information about the role and responsibilities of SMSF trustees go to **www.ato.gov.au/super**.

Recording-keeping and property ownership

For those SMSFs buying property directly, to ensure your fund records have been correctly established, your accountant or superannuation administrator will want to sight:

- a copy of the property's title;
- the purchase contract; and
- the settlement and disbursements statements.

If your fund has borrowed to acquire the property, they will also want to see:

- the loan agreement;
- the agreement to transfer the property;
- the security trust deed; and
- a letter from the solicitor who drafted the documents confirming that the requirements of superannuation legislation were followed.

For those of you who have engaged the services of an estate agent to manage property purchases you will receive an annual statement detailing monthly rental and expenses paid on your behalf.

Keep in mind that there could be other expenses SMSF trustees will have to take care of, such as insurance on the property purchased.

If you manage your investment property directly, you will also need to keep records of monthly rentals and expenses for your accountant or superannuation administrator.

Indirect property ownership record-keeping

Purchasing property indirectly usually involves the fund trustee buying into or investing in listed or unlisted property trusts and does not involve the fund purchasing the property outright. This approach is used when property is too large for a single investor and a trust is the best way to proceed.

In this scenario, investors (such as an SMSF) are not the legal owners and the title of the property is held by the trustee of the property trust, with investors simply owning units in the trust.

What record-keeping and documentation is required in this scenario?

Investors in indirect property will receive either a unit certificate or a holding statement confirming how many units are held in the trust. This is evidence of ownership of the units and is a most important document.

Keep in mind that the trustee of the property trust will receive all the income generated from the trust and pay all of the expenses. Any profits generated will then be distributed among unit trust holders (investors). All investors will receive an annual tax statement to assist with preparation of accounts and tax returns.

Distributions from smaller private trusts will typically be paid annually while those from larger public trusts could occur quarterly or half yearly.

Listed trusts and trusts offered by fund managers may give investors the opportunity to reinvest distributions. If you elect to take this course of action, you can expect to receive an updated holding statement for each reinvestment.

Your accountant or superannuation fund administrator will want to sight:

- the buy notice or application and the holding statement for the year in which the investment was made;

- distribution statements, the annual tax statement and notices showing details of units issued as a result of reinvestments for each year the investment is held.

Key Points

- If your fund does not keep adequate records proving compliance it may lose its status as a 'complying' fund and be denied the tax concessions enjoyed by complying funds.

- All records pertaining to sale and purchase of property are particularly important.

- The accounts of your SMSF will need to be audited annually.

- It is a good idea to engage the services of an accountant or superannuation specialist to help you with compliance.

CHAPTER 15

Government proposals affecting superannuation funds

DESPITE OUR politicans' promises to keep superannuation as simple as possible it still seems to be constantly changing. In April 2013, while we started working on this revised edition of the book, the Federal Government announced several changes to superannuation funds in Australia.

There are two which could have an impact on people electing to buy property via a self managed super fund. The first relates to concessional contributions.

Concessional contributions

Concessional contributions are those contributions for which a tax deduction can be obtained.

With effect from the 2013/14 year, the concessional contribution cap has been lifted to $35,000 for people aged between 59 and 74 at 30 June 2013. From July 2014 this will be extended to people aged 49 or more at 30 June 2014.

For people who are gainfully employed and are aged 75 or over, employers will be required to continue paying the compulsory superannuation contributions of 9.25 per cent of salary at July 2013. No other concessional contributions or any non-concessional contributions can be paid beyond age 75.

These changes have been legislated.

Tax on pension-paying funds

The government has announced it proposes to introduce changes to the taxation of pension-paying superannuation funds. Tax on non-pension paying funds will continue to be levied at the rate of 15 per cent.

At present pension-paying funds are completely exempt from income tax, if all of the members are in pension mode. Where a fund has pension and non-pension members, part of the fund's investment income is tax exempt.

An SMSF which has segregated assets between the two groups will continue to pay tax at the rate of 15 per cent on the earnings relating to the accumulation members. For non-segregated funds, an actuary will determine the proportion of income belonging to the two classes of members.

The government's proposals are to first split the income attributable to pension members between the pension members. Then, if any pensioner has income in excess of $100,000 in any given year, tax at the rate of 15 per cent will be levied on the excess.

Let's look at an example of how this would work in practice.

Example:

Ben and Melissa are both retired and their fund has total investment income for tax purposes of $230,000. Of this $90,000 is attributed to Melissa and $140,000 to Ben.

Under the government's proposed changes, Melissa's account in the SMSF would not be subject to tax. However, for Ben, the fund will receive a tax assessment for $6,000 being 15 per cent of the income above $100,000 threshold.

Depending on the overall size of the fund, some SMSFs will be affected each year by this proposal. Others will only be affected in some years. Ben and Melissa's fund might generate income of $150,000 the following year. If this were the case, neither Ben nor Melissa would be subject to tax on their share of the fund's income. But if they were to sell a property, the realised gains from the sale, after the one-third discount, may be sufficient to cause tax to be paid. This assumes the property was purchased after these changes came into effect.

I would stress that this change is only a proposal at the time of writing. But because it has the potential to affect the benefits that can be obtained from investing in property via an SMSF, it is best to be aware of it. It is important to note that even if it did affect your SMSF, the net return from the sale of the property would still be greater than if the property had been owned personally.

APPENDIX A:
NON PROPERTY INVESTMENTS

This book focuses on investing in property (real estate) but I am mindful that many SMSF trustees will be seeking a diversified portfolio of investments. So for completeness I have included this appendix which touches on non-property investments.

While some may dream of starting an SMSF and filling it with exotic investments like rare art works, vintage cars, yachts and racehorses, in reality few actually go down this path. Most opt for a spread of quality investments that will build a nest-egg and provide for a comfortable retirement, such as:

- Shares in listed and (in some cases) unlisted companies. There are over 2,000 companies listed on the ASX. Investors can buy and sell these shares through their SMSFs, benefitting from capital gains and in many cases franked dividends.

- Shares in listed and unlisted unit trusts. With unit trusts, the trust property is divided into a number of defined shares called units. Beneficiaries subscribe for units in much the same way as shareholders in a company subscribe for shares.

- Shares in managed funds. Also known as unit trusts, managed funds are vehicles that allow you to pool your money with other investors in a single fund, allowing you to invest in assets that might otherwise be out of reach. Managed funds can invest in a variety of assets including shares (in Australia and overseas), property and fixed interest or a combination of these.

- Fixed-interest securities such as term deposits. These are much like shares but not as volatile and open to fluctuation. You can purchase fixed interest securities in investments issued by governments, banks and other companies both locally and internationally.

- Art and collectables include cars (both real and model), jewellery and precious stones, antique furniture, even trophies. In fact, one SMSF I have had dealings with over the years had a Melbourne Cup from the late 19th century as part of its investment collection.

Sole purpose test

Whatever investment choices you make, at the end of the day, they must support you in your retirement. They must meet the so-called 'sole purpose test' which is there to ensure SMSFs are maintained strictly for the purpose of providing benefits to members when they retire or to their dependants should they die before retiring.

Basically, all fund assets must be able to generate income for your retirement. As a result you cannot use assets in your fund:

- for your own purposes;
- to loan to friends or family;
- in the running of your business;
- to buy the family home. Neither can you allow fund members or family to live in residential property purchased by your fund.

Similarly, while SMSFs can invest in jewellery, wine and art, members are prohibited from wearing the jewellery, they can't drink the wine, neither can they hang the art in their homes. However, they can rent it to an arm's length business or an art bank that rents out artwork on an ongoing basis.

If you are planning to loan art owned by your SMSF to galleries or rent them out, it is important to ensure your fund receives rent and that there is a written agreement covering matters such as rent and rental increases. You will also have to arrange an insurance policy in the name of the SMSF trustees within seven days of acquiring any new artwork or collectables.

While it might seem like a good idea to use your super to invest in art and collectables, it is worthwhile keeping in mind that these types of investments are notoriously volatile and the market for these asset classes is generally pretty illiquid.

Remember, contravening the sole purpose test could mean that your fund will no longer be eligible for valuable tax concessions and instead of your SMSF's income being taxed at 15 per cent, this could shoot up to 46.5 per cent which is what happens to 'non complying' funds.

Despite these restrictions, there is a range of interesting investments you can make with your fund, as long as you follow the rules. So, sure, have some fun with a small portion of your fund but remember that at the end of the day, your SMSF is designed to support you in retirement.

APPENDIX B:
KEY CONTACTS

Throughout the book I have made reference to the fact that is it important to obtain professional assistance as and when required. These professionals have been grouped together under the following headings.

Real estate agents

For those of you who are looking for a real estate agent to assist you with acquiring and/or managing an investment property, the state and territory institutes are:

Real Estate Institute of ACT	www.reiact.com.au
Real Estate Institute of NSW	www.reinsw.com.au
Real Estate Institute of NT	www.reint.com.au
Real Estate Institute of Queensland	www.reiq.com.au
Real Estate Institute of SA	www.reisa.com.au
Real Estate Institute of Tasmania	www.reit.com.au
Real Estate Institute of Victoria	www.reiv.com.au
Real Estate Institute of WA	www.reiwa.com.au

Solicitors

If you need a solicitor to handle either:

- the purchase or sale of a property by your SMSF; or
- the transfer of an investment property to your SMSF

the Law Society in your state can be contacted on the details below:

ACT Law Society	www.actlawsociety.asn.au
Law Society of NSW	www.lawsociety.com.au
Law Society NT	www.lawsocnt.asn.au
Queensland Law Society	www.qls.com.au
Law Society of SA	www.lawsocietysa.asn.au

Law Society of Tasmania   www.taslawsociety.asn.au
Law Institute of Victoria   www.liv.asn.au
Law Society of WA   www.lawsocietywa.asn.au

Remember, your SMSF can only obtain business real property from a fund member or an associate. This means that at the time of acquisition the premises were wholly and solely being used by a business.

Financial planners

If you require the assistance of a financial planner, you could contact:

The Financial Planning Association of Australia Limited
Website: www.fpa.asn.au

Association of Financial Advisers Limited
Website: www.afa.asn.au

Partners Wealth Group

If you would like to contact either Martin Murden or other members of the Partners Wealth Group, their details are:

Martin Murden
Email: mmurden@partnerswealthgroup.com.au

Partners Wealth Group
Website: www.partnerswealthgroup.com.au
Email: office@partnerswealthgroup.com.au
Tel. 1800 333 143

GLOSSARY OF TERMS

Accumulation phase – this is when an SMSF is 'accumulating' (or saving) money and assets for the purposes of providing an income in retirement.

Actuary – a professional who specialises in the mathematics of risk as it relates to insurance calculations and annuity rates.

Assets – property, cash and other valuables that are of some value and/or generate wealth in the form of income or capital gains.

Associate – A simple test to determine association is as follows:

- Two people would be deemed associated if they are related (e.g. family members such as brothers and sisters), or if they are involved in a business venture together.
- A person and a company would be associated if the person is a director of the company and is actively involved in the day-to-day operations of the company or if the person has over 50 per cent of the shares or voting rights for the company.
- A person and a trust would be associated if the person was a beneficiary of the trust and the trust was a discretionary trust (such as a family trust) or if the person had over 50 per cent of the units or voting rights for a unit trust.

Auditor – a professional engaged to study the financial affairs of the SMSF and check that the fund is paying the right amount of tax.

Australian business number (ABN) – an identification number allocated to a business registered in Australia.

Australian Tax Office (ATO) – Australia's national tax regulator.

Bare trust – *please see security trust.*

Beneficiary – a person entitled to receive, or who is already in receipt of, a benefit from a fund or a trust.

Benefits – in the context of superannuation these are the monies paid out (or distributed) from a superannuation fund to members and/or beneficiaries.

Business real property – property used wholly and solely for business purposes at the time of purchase. It can be a shop, factory, office or farmland. It can even be a house used for business purposes, such as a doctor's surgery or an accountant's office.

CBD – Commercial business district.

Capital gains tax (CGT) – tax payable on the profits from the sale of investment property.

CGT discounts – reduction in tax payable on capital gains. Individuals are generally entitled to a 50 per cent discount on capital gains; SMSFs are entitled to a 33.3 per cent discount.

CGT event – this is a sale (disposal) or purchase of investment property that can trigger capital gains tax obligations.

Commercial property – property used for running a business.

Concessional contributions – contributions made to superannuation using pre-tax dollars, such as the compulsory superannuation guarantee (SG). The SG is 9.25 per cent of salary, as at 1 July 2013 which employers have to pay into employees' superannuation funds.

Contribution caps – caps on the amount you can contribute to superannuation each year. You should beware of exceeding contribution caps as stiff penalties apply.

Concessional (pre-tax) contributions caps are:
- People aged 59 to 74 (as at 30/6/2013) – $35,000
- People aged under 59 (as at 30/6/2013) – $25,000

Non-concessional (post-tax) contributions are:
- People aged 65 to 74 – $150,000
- People aged under 65 – $150,000 but can bring forward the following two years.

Corporate trustee – a separate company that is set up for the specific purpose of managing an SMSF. All fund members must be directors of the corporate trustee.

Dependant – includes a spouse (current or former), a bona fide de facto, a child under age 18, and people in an 'interdependency' relationship.

Disqualified person – someone disqualified from being a trustee of a fund who has prior convictions involving dishonest conduct, and/or is insolvent, bankrupt or has entered into an arrangement with creditors under Part X of the *Bankruptcy Act 1996* or someone who has a civil penalty order under the *Superannuation Industry (Supervision) Act 1993*.

DIY – do it yourself, SMSFs are sometimes referred to as DIY funds.

Eligible termination payment (ETP) – tax may be payable on lump sum benefits that go to a non-tax dependant.

Family trust – a discretionary trust often formed to operate a business or to be used as an investment vehicle. The trustees of a family trust determine how the capital and income from the trust will be distributed among beneficiaries.

Franked dividends – dividends paid by a company to its shareholders from after-tax profits. A franked dividend carries with it an 'imputation credit' that shareholders can claim at the end of the tax year. Dividends can be 'fully franked' or 'partially franked'.

Goods and services tax (GST) – a broad-based consumption tax levied at 10 per cent on most Australian goods and services.

Income stream – in the context of superannuation this is a pension or annuity paid during retirement. It could also be a TRIS – a transition to retirement income stream – paid to people while their fund is still in the 'accumulation' phase.

***In specie* contributions** – these are contributions of property made to an SMSF, where no money changes hands. The value of *in specie* contributions is considered part of overall contributions and therefore consideration should be given to the contribution caps.

Industrial property – examples are factories or warehouses.

Interdependency relationship – is defined as a close personal relationship between two people who live together, where one or both provides financial and domestic support and personal care for the other. Two examples are a same sex couple and an adult child living with his or her widowed parent.

Interest-only loan – a loan agreement whereby only the interest payments are repaid over the life of the loan with the principal being paid out when the asset bought using the borrowings is sold.

Investment income – income generated by investments, for example, rent from a tenanted investment property, dividends from shares, distributions from unit trusts and proceeds from the sale of assets.

Investment strategy – an SMSF must have (usually a written) investment strategy outlining how the fund's assets will be invested. The fund must follow this strategy or it may be deemed 'non-complying'. The strategy must be reviewed by the trustees of the fund periodically to ensure that it best serves the fund.

Leverage – the use of borrowing to finance an investment, with the rise or fall of the value of the investment proportionally greater than comparable investments. Leverage is used to increase the potential return of an investment.

Legal personal representative – executor of your estate.

Limited recourse loan – a loan that limits the lender's recovery to the property only, leaving other assets in the super fund intact.

Listed investments – shares or unit trusts traded on the stock exchange.

Lump sum – an amount of money that can be paid out upon or during retirement. Often used to pay off a mortgage, fund a big trip or purchase a new car.

Medicare levy – currently a 1.5 per cent levy on income that pays for Australia's public health system. It is usually quoted along with the marginal tax rate. For example, the highest marginal rate of tax is 46.5 per cent (including Medicare levy). It is to increase to 2 per cent from 1 July 2014 to pay for the National Disability Fund.

Preservation age – funds are 'preserved' in a superannuation fund until preservation age when they can be accessed. Preservation age is currently 55, with later ages being phased in according to your date of birth as follows:

Date of birth	*Preservation age*
Before 1 July 1960	55
1 July 1960- 30 June 1961	56
1 July 1961- 30 June 1962	57
1 July 1962- 30 June 1963	58
1 July 1963- 30 June 1964	59
After 30 June 1964	60

Negative gearing – a common strategy used by high-income earners to save money on tax and benefit from capital appreciation of property. The way it works is investors buy a property and the rental income it generates is LESS than the outgoings (e.g. loan repayments, ongoing management and maintenance costs). This loss is offset against other taxable income.

Non-concessional contributions – contributions to super funds using after-tax dollars. These can only be made by fund members (not employers).

Non-lapsing binding death nomination – a formal document which enables you to determine who will receive your death benefit (provided they are dependants and/or your legal personal representative). This document effectively binds the trustee to following your instructions in paying your benefits.

Off the plan – a purchase agreement whereby people buy a property before construction has been completed for a price determined before the development has been completed.

Real estate investment trusts (REITs) (formerly known as property trusts) – a collective investment vehicle that either owns a portfolio of real property, such as shopping centres or office buildings or is established to acquire a single property. Investors buy units in the REIT and can buy and sell these (as they would listed company shares) in the case of listed REITs; or redeem these from the fund in the case of unlisted REITs. Units in unlisted REITs are issued by the fund manager based on the asset value of the trust and are redeemed rather than sold to another buyer.

Regulated fund – a fund is regulated by the *Superannuation Industry (Supervision) (SIS) Act* and is therefore eligible for favourable tax treatment.

Retail property – property used to run a retail business, for example a shop or cafe.

Retirement age – currently 60 years of age if you stop working, otherwise 65 (phasing in to 67) when you are entitled to receive the government age pension if you are eligible.

Retirement phase – phase of a super fund when the fund starts paying benefits to its retired members.

Reversionary pensioner – the person you nominate to receive the remaining balance of your pension account when you die. This typically would be your spouse or partner.

Roll over – to transfer money or property into a superannuation fund.

Security or 'bare' trust – a separate entity created with the sole purpose of being the 'interim' owner of a property bought by an SMSF with borrowings, until the loan has been repaid in full and ownership of the property reverts to the SMSF.

Self managed super fund (SMSF) – a trust established for one to four people. Here money is held 'on trust' principally to fund members' retirements.

Sole purpose test – according to the 'sole purpose test' an SMSF's primary purpose is to provide fund members with benefits when they retire or their beneficiaries with benefits should they die early.

Stamp duty – a tax imposed on the legal transfer of documents. This is a state-based tax.

Strata title – a form of ownership devised for multi-level apartment blocks and horizontal subdivisions with shared areas. The 'strata' part of the term refers to apartments being on different levels or 'strata'.

Superannuation Industry (Supervision) (SIS) Act – the Act that governs all superannuation funds in Australia.

Tax file number (TFN) – the number issued by the tax office to identify all taxpayers – individuals, trusts and/or corporates.

Title – legal document recording the ownership of a property.

Transition to retirement income stream (TRIS) – an income stream paid to a member who has reached preservation age and is starting to cut back their paid working hours. There are limits to the proportion of your fund that can be taken out as a TRIS each year.

Trust – a legal structure that is created to exist for a person or company to hold property for others who are intended to benefit from the property or income from that property.

Trust deed – the document governing how a trust should be managed, who it will benefit and who is to manage it.

Trustee – an individual or organisation which holds or manages and invests assets held in a trust for the benefit of another/others.

Unit trust – a trust in which investors are allocated a set number of units for their investment. For example, if each unit was valued at $1, an investor with $1,000 would receive 1,000 units.

INDEX

www.ingramcontent.com/pod-product-compliance
Ingram Content Group UK Ltd.
Pitfield, Milton Keynes, MK11 3LW, UK
UKHW031703170726
13836UKWH00001B/7